IN THE PATH OF THE WHIRLWIND

An Apprentice Guide To The World Of SAP

Michael Doane
The Consulting Alliance

In the Path of the Whirlwind

An Apprentice Guide to the World of SAP

This book was written by Michael Doane of The Consulting Alliance, with the assistance of The Consulting Alliance principals, consultants, and project managers.

ISBN 1-57579-029-7

Published by The Consulting Alliance, 101 South Main Avenue, Sioux Falls, South Dakota 57104-6423.

Printed in the United States.

Second Edition - Revised and Expanded

Third Printing, Revised

A State of the Art Information System: Your Competitive Edge?

Why is SAP So Hot and Will It Stay This Hot?

Is SAP Right for You?

After the License is Signed...What Are the Costs? All of the Costs...

Instant Gratification R/3

History of an SAP Implementation

Managing the Changes

The Future of R/3

Last Minute Notes

Q: How long does it take to implement SAP?

A: How long is a piece of string?

PREFACE

This book is addressed to anyone who is considering SAP as a long-term information systems support, whether you are a CEO or a middle manager, or what we like to think of as a visionary in the coffee room. It will also serve those who have already banged heads with an implementation process and are in search of enlightenment.

There must be a million pages of documentation for SAP R/3 and another hundred thousand PowerPoint slides reproduced on CDs, but in months of searching we were never able to find a simple tract telling simple folk just what SAP is all about. That is the purpose of this book. What it's all about.

In the press, and throughout North America, there is a wealth of hearsay and heated opinion on the subject, much of it emotion-laced due to a number of misconceptions, the most telling of which is that SAP implementations have to cost an arm and a leg and the sacrifice of firstborn.

What we are intending with this book is to cut through the smoke of the hearsay and opinions in search of what is true and what is untrue about SAP, particularly SAP R/3 (and soon enough, R/4).

This book was not written in the dark. Help came from a variety of sources throughout The Consulting Alliance, and credit must be given to Wolfgang Beitz, who brought his fifteen years of SAP experience to the interview table, to Daniel and his volumes of SAP war stories, Jim O'Keefe who has his way with words and then some, Pat Campbell who hates to see it done incorrectly, and to Barb Seder, who gave this project its initial launch into the open sea, and when it drifted too far out, helped bring it into shore.

In the final analysis, we understand that a lot of pain goes into implementing SAP R/3, but we also know that a company can LEAP into the light if the implementation is wisely rendered. A vice president we know recently talked of his company in wistful terms. Not too many years ago, his staff of hundreds lived a good life. Sales were about as brisk as they are today and the distribution flow occurred in a humane, if somewhat leisurely good ol' boy fashion. Yes, some tightening up was needed and yes, cost of sales was tilting too far northward. But this VP's distribution schemes, dictated by economic necessity AND upper management vision, have changed radically. Today, sales and distribution staff are strapped to headsets and systems that measure the length of their client calls, the delivery turnaround, and *the percentage of abandoned orders*, which have doubled in the past ten years. Something is out of whack. The company is making less money and the quality of life of its people has degraded from pleasant to purgatorial. This man knows that the *only* solution for his massive distribution network units is SAP because of its integration. Nothing else (his words) will meet the requirements, not best of breed with interfaces or internal development or bended knee in prayer. We love this man and his clarity of vision.

The consultants who have contributed to this book do not love every client, but we are unanimous in our belief in the potential of this magnificent software. Properly confronted and effectively implemented, SAP R/3 can radically better the life of a company or corporation and -why not?- better the working conditions of their employees. What a concept.

A State of the Art Information System: Your Competitive Edge?

In Search of Integrated Systems with PC Flexibility, Data Integrity, and Whatever Else We Can Think of While We Implement

The Modular Stroke Interfacing Approach of the Roaring 80's

Integrated software systems have been around since the late seventies, usually of the modular pick-and-choose variety. Companies of all sizes and activities have been able to install combinations of desired modules and interface them to legacy systems, write add-ons, or customize the software to fit specific company needs. Since this time, systems have been viewed as a series of interrelated modules, much in the same way as businesses have become increasingly compartmentalized.

Most of these systems were thought of as *integrated* because each of the business functions, from sales order entry to manufacturing to invoicing and collection were included and updates between modules were effected. The reality was that the integration of the applications was only partial. In fact, most applications were only *interfaced*, not only to whatever legacy systems were retained but also to each other. The difference between integrated systems and interfaced systems is the difference between a handshake and a postcard addressed to "Occupant". With interfacing, data is necessarily duplicated between systems. As such, real time updating is not always available and data sources can become confused.

With so many postcard systems around, data bases and communications proved to be the challenge of the decade while, in parallel, PC-based subsystems were being used to patch the holes left by the incomplete functionality of systems. Companies were installing new systems at a furious rate, while stand-alone PC information systems were producing mountains of information with spreadsheets and data base systems. The results should have been predictable. Information was too often limited to the departments that generated it. Management information, used for decision-making, was culled from a variety of sources, PC and mainframe based, and then re-manipulated on stand-alone *management* PCs. This resulting "management information system" was therefore oftimes based upon anecdotal business data.

Pump Up the Volume: Client/ Servers and the Info-PC-Stat Freak Jam

The emergence of client-server technology only accelerated the stampede toward PC usage. On client/server networks, users could not only run "company" systems but could continue to run their renegade (or 'complementary') systems AND share data and programs with other renegade systems. With so much information and so many slick new ways to express or share it (spreadsheets, report generators, slide shows, to mention a few), companies became overwhelmed with data-based points of view. These same companies began to resemble universities rather than businesses as more and more varied reports were coming down the pipeline to management and one report would contradict another or merely confuse the issue.

In the rush to create these systems, one key factor was neglected more often than not, and that was the need to maintain the integrity of the data that was flying around the network.

Further, and more to the point, a wealth of *information* was viewed as the pinnacle of success. Only recently has the concept of *workflow* begun to truly emerge as the focal point of new systems supports. The inherent link between workflow and downsizing has sparked a small systems revolution.

Grasshoppers in the Board Room

During the same years that information systems were exploding, there was a flood of new thinking about management techniques and corporate structuring, some of which was rational and some of which was ludicrous. It was common to find managers reading *The Five Minute Manager* or Lao Tzu's *The Art of War* and marking passages that might be practiced around the office. Large consulting companies were building major practices in Total Quality Management (TQM), circles of excellence, KanBan/JIT, etc. and although these fresh  approaches toward doing business were often very successful, there were no fundamental changes to the way information systems were perceived or used in a company. CEOs may have been itching to radically re-structure their companies according to advanced business principles, but they were unable to do so because of the excessive time required to acquire or develop the systems to support a radically new organization and retain client/server architecture and flexibility.

The challenge came down squarely to this: How to re-invent the company and provide the necessary IS supports in a timely fashion?

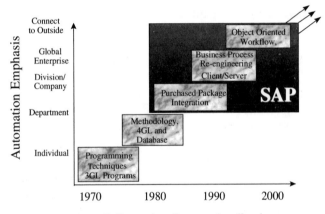

Information System Applications

In Search of a Modern Information System

A modern information system is one that delivers reliable information where needed and when needed. Simple, no? Except that this standard of information systems, in existence since Bill Gates had a five figure income, has been elusive. This isn't because systems people have been incompetent, nor can management, users, software houses, or hardware companies be blamed. And, no, we won't settle on the

4

diplomatic combination of all of the above. Quite simply, the nature of business has evolved and the management world has been slow to react to this evolution.

Until recent years, information systems were too often regarded as necessary overheads, support systems that had to be fitted together to support continuing business functions. "OK, we'll create six new sales divisions and organize them by region, merge the three factories into a single cost center, and eliminate the warehousing network. Somebody send a memo to IS and tell them to get programming started."

With the rise of business process reengineering and the consequent notion of workflow, management is beginning to see that business changes and systems changes are inherently linked. This has always been the case, but it has not always been the perception. More to the point, business staff is now more involved in systems decisions than ever before. In olden times, business staff provided 'functional specifications' to IS staff and then hoped it all worked out. Now, through business process reengineering, business staff is shaping the system in a far more direct manner.

Information systems are acquired and developed at the behest of management. They are, in a direct fashion, a *reflection* of management vision. Too often, new systems are used to support old organizations or to patch over fundamental weaknesses. As in failed war colleges, too many companies are fighting the last war instead of foreseeing the coming war.

A company losing a dollar a minute with poor information systems can lose ten dollars a minute with whiz bang information systems if the business processes supported by the whiz bang information systems are not redesigned.

Modern business long ago outpaced corporate capacity for infrastructural support. Distribution networks cross national and lingual boundaries while still attempting to provide small-town style local service. Companies seek to provide inherent links between sales, stock systems, purchasing, and manufacturing. On paper, these links are organic but in reality they are usually herk-a-jerk failures because management vision has not extended to the systems that might support them.

A 'modern information system' is one that reflects clear-minded, results-oriented, business process reengineering. Not all systems are capable of adequately supporting new business processes. But there is one system the very name of which is now synonymous with business process reengineering. SAP.

Why is SAP So Hot and Will It Stay This Hot?

Testing the Waters of the World's Number One Software

What is SAP?

Systems, Applications, and Products ...SAP. The least imaginative element of this otherwise marvelous software suite is this dull-as-dishwater name. As for its pronunciation: just as you would not say "Ibem" when referring to International Business Machines, you should not say "Sap" when referring to Ess Ay Pee.

Now that you can say it and you know what the acronym stands for, what is it? First of all, SAP AG is a supplier, a company from Walldorf, Germany. The system we will be referring to through the remainder of this book is their product R/3, as in Release 3. And what is R/3? Inhale. R/3 is a fully integrated suite of systems that support the entire range of standard business applications, incorporating state of the art client/server architecture, functional integration of its applications with PC applications, the portability of open systems, real time data updating, and the flexibility of graphical user interface (GUI) based on the Windows standard. Exhale.

Now re-read that description. It is one true sentence in a systems world filled with half truths, dependent clauses, whiz bang schematics, and miles of small print. It is also a promise, an invitation to a vision, and the potential lead-in for either a rousing corporate leap forward or a deep and dark abyss of meetings, consultant costs, rage, and failure. Because SAP R/3 is intended to take care of everything, anyone contemplating using it should be prepared to take care of everything.

But first, a short course in SAP application ID's:

CO	Controlling	
FI	Financial Accounting	
	EC	Enterprise Controlling
	IM	Capital Investment Management
	AM	Assets Management
	TR	Treasury
HR	Human Resources	
	PA	Personnel Application
	PD	Personnel Planning & Development
LO	Logistics	
	MM	Materials Management
	PM	Plant Maintenance
	PP	Production Planning
	PS	Project System
	QM	Quality Management
	SD	Sales & Distribution

Basis   The middleware which smoothes operations across the variety of possible operating systems

ABAP/4 The programming language used

Integration points being what they are, SAP parlance tends toward a concatenation of applications to describe business functions. SD-MM will refer to the inherent links between Sales & Distribution and Materials Management (e.g., materials ordering to fulfill sales orders); FI-CO refers to the cost accounting functions in accounting, MM-PP is generally what was otherwise known as MRP and MRP2. Materials Costing directly relative to Sales and Distribution activity for a given factory might fall under the heading of FI-CO-SD-MM. But you get the point. Familiarization with these acronyms will come naturally if you launch an SAP project.

The array of applications is vast but other software suites on the market offer similar applications. It is not as if SAP invented the only package for sales and distribution. In fact, for *individual* applications, you may very well find software with greater functionality than that offered by SAP. The force and advantage of SAP is that all of their applications are robust and *integrated.* And there are a number of other areas in which SAP separates itself from the pack.

State of the Art Client/Server Architecture

Client / Server is an industry term denoting the concept between the "client" who requests "service" from the "server". This might have been called Czar/Serf or King/Pawn, but those names wouldn't have passed muster with the socio-polital environs of North America. Client/server architectures are intended to satisfy system requirements at four levels at once:

- Data base server: for data base maintenance and modeling

- Applications server: for customization of applications

- Presentation server: for the expression (output) of information

- Communications

Designed with three-tiered client/server architecture, the SAP R/3 system is typically comprised of the data base server, application servers, and presentation servers. In combination with the Basis System -the foundation, or middle operating system- of the R/3 system, system services can be performed.

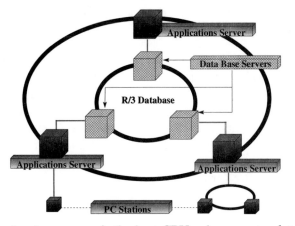

The data base server is the host CPU, where master data reside. Application modules, the R/3 kernal, are installed on the application servers, and the SAPGUI (Grapnical User Interface) resides on the presentation servers. The user will log on to SAP R/3 at his presentation server (the workstation or PC) and request the application module when he wants to process information.The application server will request data from the data base server to process the information.This design, according to industry experts, provides efficient utilization of computing resources by spreading all the components over three layers. This concept applies when organizational structures and processes can be combined into a single R/3 system.

NB: We apologize for the preceding paragraph, which has no place whatsoever in an apprentice guide.

When there are disparate organizational structures or global businesses do not map to a single R/3 system, some customers have not been able to fit into this schema. It is not unusual to find fortune 500 R/3 customers with multiple R/3 systems that do not have the same organizational structure and master data.

Even though the corporation is known as a single entity, the business processes do not fit within the confines of a single R/3 system. To its credit, SAP has devised a solution for these customers. Application Link Enabling (ALE) was developed to allow linking of multi-layer, independent data bases.

Presentation servers are responsible for the way data is seen and manipulated on screen. Most R/3 users have Windows PCs as presentation servers. Thus, the ergonomic and data base splits between company systems and PC-based systems are eliminated.

Integration of SAP Applications with PC Applications

SAP offers exceptional integration between PC applications and its own applications. Its File Transfer Service (FTS) allows data to be read and written in the presentation computer. Microsoft PC and other desktop software can use applications data, either from R/3's word processor, SAPscript or from the main SAP data base.

One stunning example of functional integration is the use of Microsoft Excel as a list viewer.

Division	Jan	Feb	Mar	Apr	May	Jun	Total
North	3	3	1	12	77	130	226
South	12	33	44	65	44	122	320
Midwest	2	5	8	55	78	233	381
West	47	67	80	95	98	133	520
England	3	5	14	22	122	211	377
France	16	23	25	47	155	344	610
Germany	0	12	6	15	44	88	165

SAP data can be accessed in Excel format. Without endangering the data base, this list data can be sorted or structured for your purposes.

Data can also be exported for use in Excel and then manipulated for reporting purposes. Exported data will not be updated back to the SAP data base, thus avoiding data pollution caused by clever but irresponsible PC users.

Throughout, SAP employs a Graphical User Interface (GUI) which gives the system a Windows feel, look, and functionality. Familiar toolbars for Editing, Viewing, Help, and such are used, as well as drop down menus. Windows-versant users will adapt easily to the ergonomic qualities of SAP.

The Portability of Open Systems

In large installations, with diverse platforms, SAP can still function with a high degree of speed and reliability. This is also true for third party applications. Most software systems should have a life cycle of around ten years, whereas hardware platforms change more rapidly. SAP's portability allows for a longer life cycle and, in conjunction with its client/server architecture, allows for growth in the number and location (i.e. platforms) of users. How this is done is the subject for a longer book. This is, after all, only an "apprentice guide".

Real Time Data Updating

SAP is not alone in providing real-time data updates. But it does stand alone in providing real time updating in an integrated fashion throughout the entire system.

The advantage this offers is breathtaking. A sales order comes in and its entry will update (depending upon configuration variables) the materials management system and/or purchasing, and/or production planning, and cash flow.

No temporary transaction files that will be updated overnight. No temporary transaction files that may be lost and have to be regenerated. And, best of all, no lag between business actions and their reflections in the data base. If SAP hears a pin drop on a shop floor, the sound will be heard in assets management.

Deutsch, Dutch, Danish Spoken Here

Though Made In Germany, SAP is the Esperanto of integrated systems, as international in feel and functionality as can be found.

The language appearing on screens, on-line help, and on-line documentation is driven by the user's log-on, as is master data that is linked to language-dependent tables. In addition to European character sets, the R/3 systems allows for pictographic display, such as the Japanese kanji or Arabic.

Thus, users in various countries can all be logged on at the same time, each working in the local language, doing the same things.

Country-specific considerations are liberally incorporated into the system, such as multi-currency handling, and tax considerations by jurisdiction (country, province, state, NAFTA, GATT, EC) and human resource requirements.

How SAP Came to Be So Hot

We don't pretend to know the secrets of the success of SAP AG. We can only trace its rise since its inception in the 1970's to its current status as "most desired" software.

The first product sold by SAP AG was a mainframe financial package that was hot stuff in Germany first, and then throughout Europe. Throughout the next decade, SAP simply added new business applications, pretty much one after another, creating a suite. A key to their ongoing success was the insistence that each succeeding application retain the same integration of its predecessors.

Finally, with R/2, the entire business spectrum had been covered and though R/2 enjoyed immense success, it wasn't until the arrival of R/3 in 1992 that the explosion occurred. The difference?   R/3 offered a three-tier client/server suite of applications *with the same high degree of integration.*

Corporate appetites for both reengineering and client/server applications being what they are, the timing couldn't have been better, particularly in the United States. The announcement of SAP R/3 with client/server and workflow coincided with the vast wave of "downsizing" (no, don't say *rightsizing* when, in all reality, these projects are nearly always intended to reduce staff) and associated methods to reduce costs. SAP is rightly seen as a means to facilitate this downsizing while upgrading client service and internal functions.

Other factors in the success of SAP are 1) its continuing devotion to research and development (25% of the annual gross revenue is plowed back into R&D, which will be discussed later in this book) and 2) its insistence on remaining a software factory, not a do-it-all corporation, offering consulting, add-on programming services, etc.

In brief, SAP came to be this hot because it fills the bill. Let's repeat the definition given at the beginning of the chapter, now with some knowledge of what it means:

SAP is a fully integrated suite of systems that support the entire range of standard business applications, incorporating state of the art three-tier client/server architecture, functional integration of its applications with PC applications, the portability of open systems to hardware and software makers, real time data updating, and the flexibility of graphical user interface (GUI) based on the Windows standard.

In short, SAP is the first and only complete applications suite with all of these desirable features. And with the worldwide shift to re-engineering of business processes, SAP figures as an essential support and long-term system partner.

The Alternatives to SAP

Given that no other complete suite of packages exists on the market, the alternatives to SAP are those traditional alternatives that have been studied for years:

1. All Home Grown Systems

2. Legacy Systems + Packages + Interfacing

3. SAP + Packages and/or Home Grown + Interfacing

Option 1 is hardly realistic in these advanced times and Option 2 is what 99% of the business world has chosen or been forced into by circumstance. Individual package software with high performance can be very desirable for specific applications, particularly industrial applications with high specificity. By the same token , home grown systems offer a certain flexibility in that they can be adapted in-house according to changing requirements. Obviously, the down side to this is the cost of that maintenance.

Option 3 has been chosen a number of times already, in which companies prefer to implement one or a number of the R/3 applications (usually Finance being one of these) in tandem with another specific package application. The impetus for such a mix is either a) prudence, in which the implementation must be of the roll-out or phased variety, or b) politics, in which a given business sector prefers to use another package and wins the boardroom skirmishes. Either way, the advantages of the integrated data base are largely lost if this option is followed.

Other alternatives, in the world of client/server competitors, are Baan, PeopleSoft, and Oracle. In 1995, these three combined had only 18% of the client/server application market, whereas SAP alone had 32%. That's why this book is about SAP. Go figure, and check out our chapter on the future of SAP for more.

How Hot is SAP?

By the end of 1995, there were well in excess of 3000 SAP R/3 installations worldwide, with North America claiming approximately 750 of them. Until 1992, when R/3 was introduced, the great majority of SAP licenses were in Europe. Since that time, as SAP support for both R/3 and English has improved, North America represents over half of SAP revenues. And that percentage is rising.

In the first six months of 1996, another 500 R/3 licenses were sold, which surpasses the rate over recent years of about 70 per month. Most software suppliers do not sell this many licenses in a year.

And SAP's growth is across the board, not only in geographic terms, but also in terms of the kinds of companies that are buying in. So many of the Fortune 500 behemoths have lumbered into the SAP tent that SAP AG has felt compelled to

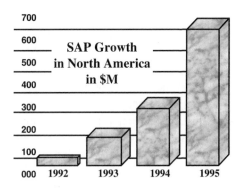

remind the rest of the world that their software is not intended only for the largest companies in the world, although nine of the ten biggest companies in the world do use SAP.

The Bum Rap on SAP AG

Of course, no company, let alone a software supplier, is perfect from top to bottom, SAP included. The recurring rap on SAP AG (the headquarters) has been a mixture of the fair, the not so fair, and the downright ugly.

A fair complaint has been the long-standing distance that SAP maintains between itself and its customers. This distance is derived from the fact that, unlike many other software vendors, SAP doesn't like to dirty itself with implementation detail, leaving that to alliance and logo partners. SAP sells licenses and thereafter maintains a support network, but both clients and associated consulting firms find that implementation support is lacking. This may change by the time this book reaches its fourth printing, particularly in America. SAP has on occasion made a concerted, renewed effort to get involved in implementation (sometimes out of exasperation with alliance partners). In the first half of 1996, a great balance of announced new tools and efforts had to do with just this subject. The wave may continued through 1997.

A not so fair complaint has to do with SAP's insistence that you must follow SAP dictates in order to succeed in implementing and using the system. Just follow the Implementation Guide and all will be well. Clients who fail to follow SAP guidelines and find themselves caught in a whirlpool of failure tend to turn around and complain about the lack of flexibility in SAP, as if the customization tools, open systems architecture, report writers, data base, and client/server do not afford sufficient room to maneuver. SAP *is* flexible at almost every level of processing. It simply takes time (and then some) to understand how to make use of that flexibility.

17

A fair and not-so-fair complaint all at once is that SAP R/3 is not a true object technology system. This is fair if the argument is the of the techno-dweeb school that says that every system must be current state of the art if it is to serve. It is a not-so-fair argument because this is clearly untrue; the 'weight' of SAP R/3 is not found in its lack of object-orientation but in the complexity of its configuring. This complexity is directly related to the vastness and totality of ambition. R/3 attempts to embrace all of business. The competitors can trumpet object technology while still fishing in shallower, and less integrated, waters. Object technology will lead to newer fishing grounds, that much is certain. And the task before SAP is to give R/3 (or probably R/4) a true object-oriented focus. But given the realities of these late 1990's, the noisy rap on SAP for not *being there* technologically is, at best, precious. This software serves.

The ugly rap on SAP is cultural. The system is viewed as German made, and therefore huge and overwhelming and filled with rules that must be obeyed *and* it dictates business processes. Or so goes the coffee room argument. Ve haf our ways. Yes. So do we all. And if nationalistic slurs and prejudices enter the stream of the project, blindness will result, and imagine into what sinkhole intended benefits will go.

The effects of blurred or fruitless business process reengineering or inept configurators are more likely at the root of any failure, not the national origin of this software.

Is SAP Right for You?

Or, a Better Question, Are You Ripe for SAP?

The Importance of a Critical Event

If you've read more than a little about SAP projects in America, you have most certainly read of companies that have failed to implement it. Failures have been explained in a variety of ways, from "the reengineering process was just too much for us" to "we trusted too much in consultants." Some honest few have come forth to admit that the failure was due to the fact that their company wasn't ripe for SAP.

Why? Because everyone was wishing, hoping, planning to put in SAP, but they were not able to do so because there was no compelling, overriding reason to do so.In short, these companies were lacking a **critical event**.

In essence, there are two types of critical events that can occur in order to provide your company with a reasonable shot at successful implementation.

The first is **survival**. If your company is falling behind the competition and an SAP implementation can turn the situation around, then implementation has a great chance of succeeding.

Failing companies do not cling to traditional methods of working; radical changes to business processes can occur without staff resistance. Failing companies do not dither in meetings; a sense of urgency can lend impetus to decision-making. Failing companies do not tinker; they sweep in change with a broadsword.

Beyond survival, the only other critical event that will help ensure a successful implementation is the declaration of intent made by a **visionary with power.** Both elements here are mandatory. The visionary must see clearly the benefits of SAP and have sufficient power to overcome company resistance, decision knots, time lags, and the like. Throughout any SAP implementation, critical decisions will have to be made by someone with the authority to back them up. The radical change of business processes does not lend itself to compromise or halfway measures. People's positions are sometimes at stake, or their career paths altered. Mini kingdoms within the enterprise are leveled, and vertical data flows are either squashed or balanced with horizontal data flows.

The obstacles to an SAP implementation are as natural as can be. Office inertia, force of habit, turf protection, fear of change, and (willful or involuntary) ignorance. Without an empowered visionary leading the effort, these obstacles may be too great to overcome.

Just as a visionary without power is a bore in the coffee room, a powerful executive without vision is a windbag in the boardroom.

It seems that the companies that need change the most are the companies that resist change the most. Change can be painful and some companies don't have the stomach for it. There is a lot of pain associated with an SAP R/3 implementation and a successful implementation can occur only if a company is prepared to embrace it.

If your company is failing AND has a visionary with power, AND a high threshold of pain, SAP R/3 can be implemented in record time.

Beyond the Critical Event (Details, Details)

Other factors, which at first glance seem to be of great import, are actually of little import in comparison:

- The size of the company: according to SAP, as of Sapphire '95, R/3 had been sold into 1105 large companies (revenues over $1B), 771 medium-sized companies ($250M to $1B), and 1337 small companies ($5M to $250M). Note: Sapphire is the annual SAP user convention in North America.

- The number of users. SAP architecture is highly flexible in this regard.

- Cost. Though discussed at length, the cost factor is either a simple price tag or an excuse for not implementing SAP, and nothing more. In reality, whatever the business initiative, upper management will make a decision that middle management will justify with a spreadsheet or two. Carrying out a cost/benefit analysis may be reassuring. Risk assessment would be more useful. Still, in order to keep your eye on the prize, a clear vision of anticipated, measurable benefits should be established.

- Time. Again, the key question is, are you compelled to implement R/3? If you are not, it may take an eternity to implement. If you are compelled, then implementation will take its swiftest course. If you are in a position to implement in an orderly (if not leisurely) fashion, why crank it up to breakneck speed? Misplaced dynamism can be more destructive than lethargy. All the same, some large but not behemoth companies have drafted five and six year plans for R/3 implementations, which strikes us as indecisive.

You may have more doubts about your own company than about SAP itself. A failed implementation could be the worst possible scenario and alibis can be readily found in the consultants, the software, the integration. You name it and it will appear on a memo headed "What Went Wrong?"

Only the firm resolve of upper management can carry a company through the hardest periods in an implementation and assure that the memo need never be written.

Your company may not pass muster. Here are some signs to watch for:

1. If top management is weak or uncoordinated or divided on which, if any, business processes to change, hold off on launching an SAP implementation. If the impetus behind an implementation doesn't come from top management with the business vision, there is little chance of success. Key decisions will be bottle-necked and the project will stall.

2. If the various divisions, or business elements, are highly independent or free-wheeling, resistance to SAP could derail the project, or at best slow it to a snail's pace.

3. If the nature of your business doesn't fall under the application suite offered by SAP, which, let's face it, is first and foremost geared (in its entire array) to a manufacturing outfit. Cross-industry applications, such as pharmaceuticals, health care, and automotives may flourish with SAP, but companies with highly specialized applications may not. All the same, these highly specialized applications are often sacred cows with less strategic benefit than they are worth. The specialization may be derived from company traditions and working methods, and a radically new approach may be more profitable.

4. If management or line staff expectations are for a "quick fix", then either SAP should be reconsidered or the implementation plan should be reviewed. Even in the best of circumstances, SAP is not implemented overnight.

If you fit into any of these categories, you should address your problems with vigor before implementing SAP.

If SAP Means 'Shoot a Programmer' To You, Maybe You Have Missed Something Vital

Failed implementations in North America have tended to follow similar scenarios, all of which have to do with a lack of upfront understanding of the nature of an SAP implementation. The most damaging misunderstanding has to do with what the customer is buying. Too many companies assume they are buying software. Well, hmm... Yes, SAP R/3 is software. It even says so on the license. But an SAP R/3 implementation leads a company down a longer, wider, yellow brick rutted road than would a simple software implementation.

Consider this simplified scenario:

1. The client has too little understanding of what SAP R/3 is all about. Big ambitions lead to an acquisition of the Big Software, so a Big Consulting Company is called in, and of course a Big Platform Supplier. Invoices flood in.

2. Business process reengineering commences. And continues. And continues. Timescales slip because they were established according to traditional software implementation assumptions. The BPR phase is a failure because of...see point 1, first sentence.

3. The client begins to understand the true nature of an SAP implementation. It is really (BPR + configuring + change management + training), and not, as the client thought, (installation + enhancements + interfacing + training).

4. The client starts over, with a fresh and enlightened point of view. Or quits and...

5. ...blames the software and writes a shrill article for a trade magazine.

The result of companies following this scenario is:

1. longer implementation periods
2. higher implementation costs
3. more shrill articles in trade magazines and newspapers.

This debacle can be very simply sidestepped if companies contemplating SAP R/3 will invest some time and cash in orienting themselves to SAP R/3 *prior* to signing a license and engaging a consulting firm or three. Such orientation may lead upper management to decide NOT to go with SAP R/3. Caveat emptor, hey. The software, hardware, consulting, and training cost so much that you'd think such orientation (at upper management level at the least) would be mandatory. A similar, and necessarily deeper, orientation should occur for these three levels of a company, preferably prior to the signing of documents:

Level 1:   C level (CEO, CIO, CFO, E-I-E-I-O)

Level 2:   Critical success staff, i.e. those who will be entrusted with making it all work

Level 3:   IS staff (or IT, or EDP, or whatever your company calls it).

Adequate orientation will **reduce confusion** as to project aims, **reduce subsequent consulting costs** because the consultants won't have to spend half their time telling your staff what the project isn't about, **reduce implementation timescales** because key players will start out on the same page, and **reduce aggravation**, which, all by itself, is worth the cost.

If you think you know how to drive and are simply getting a newer, faster, shinier car, think twice. It is not a car you are buying, nor the road, but the destination. Invest in a map. Ask directions. Get home safely. Bon voyage.

Hot Tip

Orientation of this type is becoming easier to find. This book is one example. Ask the authors about what else you might do besides read this thing cover to cover and mark the margins with witty comments. We may not be able to provide all that you will need, but we know who can.

A Note About Company Size

The American market for SAP has thus far been in odd contrast to the market elsewhere in the world. Roughly 70% of the R/3 installations in North America are in very large companies, whereas only about a third of the other installations worldwide are in very large companies. We don't know how to explain this, but are convinced that it is not because SAP is geared only for huge enterprises. Smaller and mid-
sized companies can and should give SAP a closer look, although there are a number of factors to take into account.

1. Smaller companies can't pay huge license fees, but SAP caters to this fact with its pricing structure, which is largely based upon the number of users.

2. Smaller companies can't pay $2 or $3 in consulting fees to every $1 spent on software

   AND

3. Smaller companies can't as easily allocate in-house staff full time to SAP implementation projects

   BUT

4. Smaller companies will often find business process re-design to be vastly simpler, thus radically reducing consultant requirements.

One implementation scenario to consider for such companies is remote configuration:

- consultants arrive with 100 or so of the basic business processes already configured, confirm these with your staff, and then begin the reengineering of more exotic processes

- your staff reviews and approves the process designs

- off-site, consultants configure the system as specified, leaving your staff to do their necessary jobs

- the consultants return with a prototype for your approval

- throughout the project, your staff receives SAP training at the various bootcamps that are available so that once the system is up and running, you will be in a position to drive it yourselves.

The North American trend in SAP installations may only be a two or three year blip. As more experienced consultants become available, it is probable that smaller and mid-sized companies will begin to catch the wave as well, just as they have in Europe and elsewhere. In 1993, there was only a small pool of SAP know-how in North America. The waves of capable consultants are hitting the beach with increasing regularity.

As it stands, SAP America is gearing up for a greater wave of small to mid-size installations by hiring a new sales staff and attempting to find ways in which the system can be implemented without such a heavy investment in consulting. All the same, there is so much business in the Fortune 1000 market that these small to mid-size companies will have to find help amongst the small to mid-size consulting companies specializing in SAP implementations.

After the License is Signed...What Are the Costs? All of the Costs...

What are the Real Costs of SAP?

First the Easy Part: Hardware and Software

A number of factors impact the total cost of an SAP implementation. First of all, for the license alone, you have to consider:

- number of users (some companies have as few as 10 users; Robert Bosch GmbH will have 15,000)

- type of license (single site, multi-company, global, et al)

- the number of modules chosen.

Beyond the license, a company has to consider the scope of the implementation as it pertains to company strategy and objectives. SAP AG claims that for an implementation without reengineering, the costs will be distributed equally between hardware, software, and consulting (i.e. 1/3 each). This would have to assume that no custom development needs to be accomplished to complement the SAP applications, a very unlikely proposition.

Beyond customization, many companies have wrestled with the question of whether or not SAP will function as they want it to. Clients are often convinced that certain desired functions are not available on R/3 and engage in costly design and add-on development sub-projects, only to find later that R/3 would do what they wanted all along. They just didn't know SAP well enough when they made their decision.

Prior to launching any add-on development sub-projects, be sure to adequately assess SAP customizing and configuration options. Chances are you'll find that SAP can provide functions and processes you are seeking. In this same vein, think twice about changing the base SAP code. Areas of the software that may be freely changed include "user exits". Any modifications to the software outside of these areas could have a negative impact on functionality and would definitely hamper consequent system upgrades.

More typical projects include reengineering business processes rather than customizing. It is this factor, in addition to the sometimes mind-boggling complexity of an SAP configuration, which drives consulting costs higher (think 'scope creep' and see 'consultants').

Hardware costs tend to rise according to the elaboration of the three-tier client/server system and the resulting longer-term costs of maintaining that client/server. As users and user groups are added to the system, these costs multiply. Mid-term planning and longer-term planning should be established so that you can get a handle on these costs. If all you do is slot in the one-time costs, you will be dragged before the board within a year or so after project launch and flogged.

Now the Hard Part - Consulting and Reengineering

Caught in a Consulting *Whirlwind*

Whatever the charms of R/3, there are associated costs, primarily in consulting and training, that can drive the cost of an R/3 implementation higher than many clients were prepared for. It is said that a classical (i.e. non SAP) system implementation will cost $2 of consulting for every $1 of licensing, yet SAP consulting costs have been cited as anywhere from this $2 to $1 to as high as $8 to $1.

Given this commercial and technical whirlwind, it is no wonder that the consulting firms are scrambling to find experienced SAP consultants. The trouble is, the demand radically exceeds the supply. Why? Because SAP R/3 is a unique system in many ways, distancing itself from all other software in terms of its operating base (Basis middleware), its own programming language (ABAP/4), and its high degree of

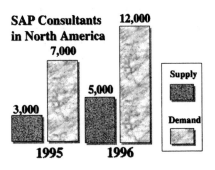

application/process integration, to name only a few of its distinctions. The predecessor to R/3, unsurprisingly named R/2, was a big hit in Europe throughout the 1980's. Thus, there has been no parallel European whirlwind, nor a parallel shortage of consulting expertise. Consultants with R/2 background can adapt to R/3 with relative ease. The problem for North America? Prior to 1993, there was only a minimal base of R/2 consultants, and by the time you read this, they have all long since been snapped into R/3 implementation projects and you have little chance of finding them for your project.

Initially, the larger consulting firms -the Big Six and others- were seen as the obvious consulting and implementing partners for SAP. However, with no base of R/2 consultants to draw upon, even these firms have been hard pressed to find enough experienced consultants to fill the needs of their clients, though their brochures claim otherwise and their track records would make Carl Lewis blush with shame. Building a Total Quality Management practice requires a proliferation of PowerPoint slides, some fancy footwork, and a busy invoice writer. Building a viable SAP practice is another story altogether.

Given the scope of the SAP market, no one consulting group can fulfill all of the identified requirements. Middle-sized companies, to name one sector, are not always in the cities that the larger firms cater to. Further, SAP implementations do not follow the classical methodologies that these large firms have followed through the past dozen years. Stalled or failed implementations have been frequent and, unfairly in many cases, SAP itself has been given the blame.

The fact is, most SAP R/3 implementation failures are due to two factors:

- the client failed to understand the scope of an SAP R/3 implementation

- the R/3 expertise that was engaged was not sufficiently 'expert' and both the product and concept were misinterpreted.

32

Despite these failures, firms are still galloping to snap up R/3 and catching up quickly with the learning curve. They have learned to distinguish real from theoretic (or converted) expertise and where to locate the real deal. They have learned not to simply dial for the major firms, but to look past them for SAP-related smaller firms, either as first-line consulting corps or as partners in the process.

Why Should I Use Consultants?

SAP is a software factory, not a consulting firm. Rather than try to gobble up the whole market pie, SAP has wisely entrusted implementation assistance to the wide world of consulting firms. These are divided into:

- Technology and Platform Partners, such as IBM, Digital Equipment, and Hewlett Packard

- Alliance Partners, which are divided into Logo Partners (such as the Big 6 consulting firms and selected others), national implementation partners, and a number of regional implementation partners.

All of the partners, and SAP itself, offer consulting services for SAP installations, implementations, and training. This mechanism of partnership is SAP's way of maintaining some kind of influence over the quality of consulting while allowing it to concentrate on the software itself and not become overwhelmed by post-license issues.

The emergence of SAP in America has been a boon to these firms because of the widespread and sometimes massive need for clients to turn to consultants for implementation and post implementation assistance.

It is safe to say that no company contemplating the implementation of SAP can avoid the use of outside consultants with SAP background. Traditional systems consulting will be of limited value. Why? Because the skills and expertise required to effectively implement SAP are at variance with the skills and expertise that most companies have traditionally relied upon. System architecture, functionality, integration, even the programming language, are unique to SAP, and the systems development and enhancement experiences previously undertaken by the company provide little benchmark experience for an SAP project.

A company *could* attempt to forego the use of consultants by providing extensive training to its own staff prior to implementing, but this would be disruptive to on-going business, not to mention to the careers of those involved. This might work if continuous training is offered to the in-house SAP staff,but the implementation process can be lengthier than many of your people are prepared for. Try telling your ace sales manager that he's about to take a year, or two, or three, off his job to learn SAP and help the company implement. Burnout happens in most implementations. It can be endemic to SAP implementations.

An SAP implementation is more business intensive than IS intensive. For implementations of "normal" systems, the team may be composed of 70% IS staff and 30% business staff. The time burden in such project, and where bottlenecks normally occur, is on the IS side, and such bottlenecks can be eased by bringing in specific technical help for a specified period.

SAP implementations, however, turn that figure on its head as projects tend to use 30% IS staff and 70% business staff. Further, IS staff is no longer in the business of designing and building the system according to business specifications. Rather, IS people assist in the configuring process being led by business staff. SAP, with its high degree of integration, takes care of the data flow, leaving implementation teams the wherewithal to concentrate upon business flows.

What Should Consultants Provide and How Fast Can We Get Rid of Them?

Consultants provide experience with SAP to shorten the user and IS learning curve and accelerate the project delivery. Their experience with projects of this breadth and complexity reduces the risk of the project. Consultants provide project methodology, project tracking, techniques for executing the project and they understand the methodology and tools that are inherent to SAP.

Consultants should best be used to facilitate not only the implementation but the company's transformation to an SAP environment by accomplishing a **knowledge transfer**. For such a transfer to successfully take place, a rough equivalence of one consultant to one in-house person should be envisioned, bearing in mind that the consultant will disappear once the transfer of knowledge has occurred.

If, at some point just before Day One use of SAP, your company's staff is self-reliant in terms of the uses and techniques of SAP configuring and business modeling, then you might conclude that judicious use of consultants has taken place. If, however, your company is still reliant on consultants, then either the consultants have failed, or are clinging to their positions on the project, or you have not sufficiently achieved the transfer of knowledge. The fault can also be that in-house staff is just not picking up the reins; again, leaving it to the experts.

How Much Do Consultants Cost?

Depending upon your company's commitment to accelerating the transfer of knowledge, consulting costs can run anywhere from two to (hold your breath) *ten* times the cost of the software itself. Thus, if you have committed a million dollars toward SAP licenses, be prepared to write another few million in checks (or a few million more, or, what the heck, yet another million more) for consulting services.

To avoid embarrassment and a company maelstrom, you first have to measure what your needs are. Are you contracting for implementation assistance alone and are you committed to investing in-house staff to keep outside costs down? If so, you will be closer to the two-to-one ratio. Are you also contracting for strategic advice, advanced user training, system add-ons to be developed in ABAP/4, and customized reporting to satisfy the professional quirks of your brilliant but eccentric CFO? Is your staff reluctant to take the reins of the project and prefers, instead, to "leave it to the experts"? In either of these latter cases, prepare yourself for a four or six or eight to one ratio.

The entire notion of "consulting costs" is somewhat simplistic to begin with, as if those costs are discrete and the only costs beyond

CONSULTING RATES	Per Day
Big Six Partner	$2500 - $4500
Project Leader	$2000 - $3000
Senior Consultant	$1500 - $2200
Module Consultant	$1200 - $1800
ABAP Programmer	$ 800 - $1600

hardware and software. In any implementation project, the amount of work to be done is finite and measurable and can be accomplished either by outside consultants or your own "inside" consultants, who are not free of charge, either.

Consider a team of implementers comprised of 50% outside consultants and 50% internal consultants (heretofore referred to as implementers). If your company salary structure isn't far beyond

	Daily OUTSIDE	Daily INSIDE	Salary + Costs
Manager	2000	800	176000
Process Mgr	1500	600	132000
IS Manager	1200	600	132000
BASIS	1000	500	120000
ABAPS4	800	400	90000

the pale, you will find that outside help costs twice as much as inside help. If your inside implementers are half the team, then your consulting costs will be only two-thirds of the total.

Other costs associated with consultants which are usually glossed over, forgotten, or swept under the rug, are:

1. office space (for meetings and deep thinking)

2. materiel (laptops, printers, desks etc.)

3. expenses (travel usually, Holiday Inns, National Car Rental, and such).

This last point is always thorny on the subject of consultants, but maybe more so for experienced SAP consultants because of their relative scarcity. Even if your company is in a populous metropolitan area, it is doubtful that the exact numbers and types of consultants you need will be locally available. For key project positions, you may find it necessary to fly consultants to and from home on a weekly basis. This is obviously not advisable on a grand scale, but for the hard-to-find one or two persons, it should be considered. We know of one consultant who flies from Canada to Georgia on a weekly basis and the client couldn't be happier. This man is a whiz at Plant Maintenance and is fast becoming a world-class connoisseur of downtown Atlanta hotels.

The Incredible, Invisible, and Very Real Cost of Training

One of the worst surprises of a blind SAP implementation is the cost and breadth of training required. In classical systems projects, training is viewed primarily as "end user training", i.e. applications training for those who will be pushing the buttons.

Since SAP implementations are business projects, and with a far wider scope than systems projects, training is not limited merely to end users. I once asked a project manager, nearing the end of an implementation, how much  had been spent on training, and his response was an immediate "a quarter of a million". Given that the entire project budget was in the multi-millions, his response was surprising, but it turned out that he was only counting the company's bills for specified outside training. Upon further investigation, we found that the real cost of training was somewhere between $1M and $1.5M, of which only a fraction had been allocated to end user training.

A successful project should include these levels of training (somewhat in the order in which they would occur):

BEFORE ACQUISITION OF R/3

1. Your first training cost is occurring just now, you are reading this book.

2. Staff/management orientation. Prior to signing the license and installing hardware, you should have a serious orientation to SAP R/3. Read on for details.

AT ACQUISITION:

1. Project management training. Whoever you assign as the internal project manager should be trained to the project methodology that your consultant(s) will be using throughout the implementation.

2. IS Training - Basis and ABAP/4 for the IS staff that will still be around after the implementation is finished.

3. Client/server, network, techie stuff with costs that add up. Not even small companies can avoid the necessity of having at least some in-house client/server expertise.

4. Business process reengineering - concepts and methods. Your project staff should have a solid grasp of this rather than leaving it to the consultants, who, after all, do not know your business as well as you do.

THROUGHOUT THE PROJECT

1. SAP Applications training for those who will be direct users.

2. Transfer of knowledge. Within the context of the project, your staff will be learning about R/3 from the consultants. This is only one area where 'training' costs overlap with 'consulting' costs.

3. Change Management. This is the most difficult cost to estimate because training is required according to the results of your business process reengineering:

- new procedures will require job re-training for much of your staff
- new job training should occur for staff that is displaced by the BPR
- everyone will have a certain moment or phase of flipping out...new methods, new faces, new furniture, happy face stickers on pink slips and the like.

The most difficult training aspect to measure is this last. In some large projects, a consultant will be assigned full-time to just this sector, but the majority of project leaders tend to

ignore change management entirely. The perils of this
ignorance are explored later in this book.

Why is the Demand for SAP Expertise Outpacing the Supply? And How Does this Affect Project Costs?

SAP only took off in the U.S. after the introduction of R/3 in
1992. Both SAP and its Alliance Consultants were unprepared
for the explosion of business and have never caught up.

Why not? First of all, there is no substitute for experience and
this is especially true for the world of SAP. There was a wealth
of expertise in R/2 outside the U.S., and the consulting firms
merely had to upgrade their capabilities to embrace R/3 to take
advantage of the opportunities.
Until the arrival of R/3, U.S.
consulting firms that supported
SAP were limited. And with the
R/3 explosion, there was no pool of experienced R/2 people to
draw upon in the U.S..

Despite the well-documented shortage of experienced SAP
consultants, companies are going ahead with their implementations…and scrambling to find good help. This obviously
drives up the rates for SAP consultants worth their salt. People
with as little as one year of experience with SAP, and often
with that year's experience being limited to a single function,
are being billed as 'senior' consultants.

The effect that all this has on project costs cannot be
overstated. Consulting costs are up because of the high
demand for SAP expertise. Further, reengineering is not
something that comes naturally or easily to most companies,
most particularly very large enterprises with a high degree of
vertical organization. The notion that SAP is hugely expensive
comes from the experiences of companies going through a
painful, lengthy, and costly, process redesign.

Consultants can lengthen the project if they are not directed to get at the heart of your requirements. On the other hand, consultants can help speed up the process by breaking down resistance to SAP within your organization. They can view the process redesign with fresh and objective vision, and provide SAP expertise and training for the long haul. We have read articles offering the simple advice that the only consultants needed are a project manager (a good one, whether fully versed in SAP or not) and a configuring specialist. This is sound advice only if your staff is prepared to take the reins for the application implementations, SD, MM, PP, and all the rest. And if that's the case, you don't need to read this book. Set it aside, kick back.

If you're thinking of waiting to implement SAP once the consulting costs go down, it will be a long wait. With the number of new licenses sold each month in the U.S., demand for the few experienced consultants continues to rise. Don't take my word for it. Look around and see how many truly qualified SAP consultants rear their heads. Resumes are peppered with SAP acronyms, but be sure to read the dates.

Our best advice is that when you find some good SAP consultants, pay them what the market asks for, then make certain that your own staff will work elbow to elbow with them so that you will rapidly have an in-house source of SAP background.

One caution: consider motivating your own staff as they become versed in SAP. These days, a few years of experience on a project may qualify them as SAP consultants and they will probably take that experience elsewhere. A preponderance of worthy SAP consultants comes from places where the system has already been implemented.

The most successful SAP implementations are characterized by a mastery of consultants by client staff, with a firm eye on:

- managing the scope of the project,

- verifying the expertise of oncoming consultants in the early stages of the project, and

- accelerating the transfer of knowledge.

The project objectives should not be overshadowed by a concern about consultant costs. If a high ratio of consulting nevertheless assures your company of reaping the benefits of SAP, you will still come out ahead.

They're Everywhere! (What to Watch For)

The level of assistance you receive from consultants is up to you and not them. You can configure your project team with a mix of qualified consultants placed in their proper slots, or you can throw an army of consultants at the problem and hope for the best. The companies that cite consultants as the cause of implementation failure should look homeward. Following are some things to watch for when configuring your team.

Consultants may not be as experienced as advertised and are thus receiving on the job training at the expense of the client. This is a particularly common occurrence for SAP jobs in North America for two reasons; first, because SAP is a relatively new system here and experienced SAP consultants are hard to find; second, the high demand for bonafide experience in SAP has pushed the costs ever higher. Greed has set in in too many quarters and truly inexperienced consultants are being pushed into projects.

Management consultants may propose add-on activities or sub-projects which seem attractive at the outset but may be of dubious value to the defined project. In this same regard, project over runs are, sadly, in the best interests of some consulting firms. The longer the project, the higher the billing.

Whether intentional or not, consultants may widen or change the scope of the project, particularly in the course of long term projects, during which the client situation is continuing to evolve.

Large consulting firms normally have their own in-house methodologies, especially for systems projects. At times, the client is charged for use of these methodologies.This is reasonable only if the methodology applies to the defined project. To our knowledge, the only existing methodology for SAP implementation is the SAP Implementation Guide, which in itself is incomplete (as it says, a *guide* not a methodology). Other methodologies are for classical design, development, and implementation projects and would not be efficient for use in an SAP implementation.

When more than one consulting group is retained, clashes as to project methods and tools may arise. Project tasks devoted to proving the advisability of one method over another add little value to the defined project.

Clients can become dependent upon outside consultants, beyond the scope of the project, if SAP knowledge isn't transferred from consulting staff to client staff. Very efficient consultants may tend to accomplish the work themselves, for the sake of time and efficiency. Without an adequate transfer of SAP knowledge, the presence of outside consultants may be extended well beyond the completion of the defined project.

Project deadlines can slip and clients tend to wonder if these slippages are caused by consultant staff or their own staff. In some cases these slippages are due to optimistic allocations of client staff in the master plan, in other cases because of consultant mistakes or oversights. Consultants tend to presume the former.

At the outset of a long term project, the project plan is based upon anticipation and past experience. Through the long duration, many tasks that were planned become pointless and yet are carried out because they were included in the plan. Consultants may see the completion of these tasks as a contractual obligation. Cancel the tasks and re-direct resources.

The net result of any or all of these failures is additional cost to the client as well as probable delays in deadlines.

Consultants, the Suspect Orphans of the Nineties

This book is supposed to be about SAP but we seem to be spending a long time on the subject of consultants. This is because SAP implementations always entail the use of consultants and the majority of the costs fall under this heading. It is a fact that the North American consulting world has largely fallen short in the realm of SAP.

Until the eighties, consultants had a more positive image in North America. Prior to the Reagan Years, a consultant was thought of as someone who had fought the business wars for a number of years and, upon reaching middle age and hard-hewn wisdom, was prepared to offer accelerating, exhiliarating advice to companies or innoculate them from their own stupidity.

With the massive rollouts of the eighties, during which hundreds of thousands of people were downsized out of their jobs, businesses began to 'rent' employees in ever greater numbers. Displaced executives, unable to find new positions, began to hang out their shingles as 'consultants'. Some were the real deal, others were just hanging on in a world grown colder and stranger by the season. In addition to displaced executives are consultants who come straight from college, clothed in textbook theory and shiny shoes, and devoid of either scars or wisdom. I started my own career as an Olsten temp, a typist/clerk at $4 an hour in 1973. At the time, I didn't think of myself as anything more than a typist. Today, I could print up letterhead describing myself as an Alphabetic Engineer and would be certain to find work at twenty times that rate.

Consultants have become the scourge of most companies, and wrongly so. There exists today a confusion between those who truly can infuse a company with help and those who are merely...Alphabetic Engineers. And this confusion has led most people to suspect all consultants to be charlatans. It is almost to the point where you can listen to the siren song of a consultant and get downsized yourself. And become a consultant. The meaning of this becomes vague, so let's scurry back to the point that needs to be made.

In the SAP market, there are certainly a number of charlatans. This was especially the case in 1992-1995. But serious SAP assistance does exist in a number of arenas and can be found with a little digging. In simplistic terms, you will look to the Big 6 and if you are in a Fortune 100 company, there will certainly be a score of VPs to slap you on the back for it. Playing it safe has its merits. But if you want to find serious help, in real numbers, you might look to the next tier, to those companies that specialize in SAP.

Somewhere beyond the logo, beyond the box-arrow-box methodologies, these reliable companies do exist, more and more, as time goes by, because SAP has become a kind of whale upon which other marine life can be sustained. You can tell consultant jokes to each other at the water cooler and pass the time if you like. Or you can hit the phones and ask a few questions, such as those included herein. There will be no infomercials to guide you. Cher probably thinks SAP is a tree-based facial creme. Don't be downhearted. Seek us out. We are not waiting. We are busy doing service in the world of companies who know what they need.

The Toy

We are searching for simplicity now, a moment of clarity after this waterfall of advice. Where, you are wondering, does your company fit into the cost scheme? Is there a visionary in your upper management or has R/3 been foisted on you by a parent company? Is your staff already BPR-savvy, or are the majority of your colleagues the kinds of people who get better TV reception by arranging the tin foil on their antennae? Are your directors insisting that you maintain cherished legacy systems in place of some of the R/3 applications? Will you implement all at once (Big Bang) or in an orderly domino fashion (Rollout)? What are the project environment factors that will most impact the costs?

Behold, "the Toy". Toys can be tools or they can just be play objects. It depends on what sandbox you're using, who your playmates are, and, especially, your intent.

This Toy is *intended* to give you a thumbnail cost estimate for an R/3 implementation project. A complete Toy is on the last page of this chapter. We have already filled in the variable data to describe a company that will have between 400 and 500 users, on two sites, will retain four legacy systems, and implement in rollout fashion. Both its management and staff are roughly average in both commitment and skills for the job at hand. Business process reengineering will be of average duration and scope.

Their direct costs (license and hardware) will run between $4M and $5M, and indirect costs (consulting, training, internal costs) will be $12M to $15M. Total project costs = $16M to $20M.

Run this exercise for your own company, but don't trust only one person to provide the variables. Instead, have several people from your company run the exercise independently and then all of you can meet and compare your results. The odds are that despite variances in assigned weights, you will still find yourselves within 10% of each other's estimates.

How the Toy Works

First, those Direct Costs:

We assume that you will have a cost of $10,000 per user. SAP has a number of definitions for users, but in essence, you should be thinking of those brave souls who will be touching the system on a regular basis, and discount the more passive users, those who might, on occasion, run a screen query, for example.

This $10,000 can be as high as $12,000 or as low as $8,000 depending upon how well you negotiate with SAP and how much shiny new hardware you are in need of. You can therefore be conservative in your estimate by plugging in $12,000 or you can be wildly optimistic by plugging in $8,000. If you are only implementing FI-CO and SD, then you are closer to $4,000 or maybe even $3,500.

At any rate, the variables you are to provide are the minimum number and maximum number of planned users. Multiply these figures by the amount you have chosen to apply per user. The results are your minimum and maximum direct costs.

Now, those Indirect Costs:

It is up to you to assess your situation according to each of the following criteria and assign a score that reflects your assessment.

- Management (35%): this refers to the level of unity and commitment of your top management to see that R/3 is implemented. As should be obvious throughout this book, management commitment is clearly the most important element in keeping project costs down and assuring final project success. Rate this as strong (1) through weak (5).

- Staff (25%): this refers to the level of readiness and availability of the project team to be assigned, as well as the level of power that these people will have throughout the project. Rate this as strong (1) through weak (5).

- BPR Load (10%): you must estimate how radically your company will change in the course of business process reengineering. Large companies with a high degree of vertical structuring will necessarily take longer than those with more horizontal organizations. If you intend to implement R/3 on practically an as-is basis, your BPR load would be scored a 1, and if so, you might reconsider R/3 as the answer to your prayers because you have possibly misunderstood the premise. Rate this as heavy (1) through weak (5).

- Big Bang or Rollout (10%): Rollout implementations require either a more concerted transfer of knowledge on the part of project staff or more weeks added to project timescales. As scary as Big Bang implementations can be, their costs are somewhat lower. Score a 2 for Big Bang or a 3 for Rollout.

- Legacy Interfaces (10%): for each system you intend to keep and, therefore, interface to R/3, add one to this column. We are referring to full applications, not small sub-systems.

- Number of sites (10%): for each different site at which a significant number of users will be, add one to this column.

Note that the total weight of these criteria is 100%. If you disbelieve the Toy, fair enough, you can toggle the weights, but this is NOT ADVISABLE. Weight x Score equals Ratio for each of the criteria and the total ratio is your multiplier.

Multiply those minimum and maximum Direct Costs with the multiplier and your results are Minimum Total and Maximum Total Costs.

If you rated management anything worse than a 2, you might not want to post those scores on the department bulletin board next to the ads for day care or car waxing services, but you will want to review the results with a cautious eye. It is for good reason that a hefty balance of the weighting falls into this category. As you wander toward a decision regarding SAP, introspection is an ally, not a detriment.

Toy or tool or weapon? It's up to you.

The Toy
an example

A. Direct Costs

Per User= $10,000

	NUMBER OF USERS		LICENSE & HARDWARE	
	Min	Max	Min	Max
	400	500	$4,000,000	$5,000,000

B. Indirect Costs

	WEIGHT	SCORE	RATIO	KEY
Management	35%	3	1.05	Strong 1, Weak 5
Staff	25%	3	0.75	Strong 1, Weak 5
BPR Load	10%	3	0.30	Heavy 5, Light 1
Big Bang or Rollout	10%	3	0.30	BB 2, Rollout 3
Legacy Interfaces	10%	4	0.40	Number
Number of Sites	10%	2	0.20	Number
SCORING TOTAL	100%		3.00	RATIO/OTHER COSTS

C. Total Costs

	Minimum	Maximum
A. Direct	$4,000,000	$5,000,000
B. Indirect	$12,000,000	$15,000,000
PROJECT TOTAL	$16,000,000	$20,000,000

50

Instant R/3 Gratification

A Scenario for Rapid Acquisition, Training, and Implementation of SAP

Grab the Software *Before* Designing the Processes

If you have already decided to go ahead with SAP, skip this section and go on to the implementation guidelines. If you are still looking for the right software solution and SAP is only one of your options, read on.

Traditionally, companies in need of new software systems have followed a left-to-right path: 1) design the new business processes then 2) find the package that fits them most closely. In the same tradition, it is presumed that no package will fit 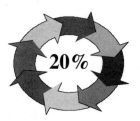 more than 80% of a company's needs, and so the remaining elusive, unique-to-you, 20% has to be designed and developed separately.

Too often, companies have failed to forge ahead with new software acquisition because of an obsession over that 20%. Instead of looking at the broader picture of how a new and dynamic 80% solution will improve company performance, they have waited, or searched for a package that just might do it all.

Besides the dithering, it is the design process (or the drafting of detailed specifications) that has traditionally slowed system acquisition and implementation. You know the scenario: you huddle with your systems people, putting pencil to paper, defining how your systems should work for you, then you go out and visit the vendors to see if there isn't a package that will fit, find that there aren't any, reconsider your specification, settle on a vendor, and then simultaneously acquire the new software and develop the missing 20% and *then* write the interfaces to any surviving legacy systems *as well as* the 20% you've developed to fulfill the specification.

The theory is that you will now have 100% satisfactory systems, meeting the needs as specified way back when.The fact of the matter is that you will have perhaps a 90% fit because a) business requirements are constantly changing and b) you have a data base that is interfaced, not integrated.

In sum, much of the specification writing/design has been redundant to the far more elaborate designs of the vendors and is largely wasted time.

Until recently, there wasn't much way around that scenario. But with the availability of integrated package suites and client/server technology, data access and presentation are no longer an issue. And with SAP, the applications themselves are both flexible and comprehensive.

The point is, you should now reconsider the traditional approach to package acquisition. Don't look for a package to support your design, look for a package suite that will be a platform upon which you will reengineer your company. And in the case of this exercise, that package suite will be SAP.

What are the Implementation Steps?

If you stick around an SAP environment long enough, you will undoubtedly hear certain phrases repeated over and over again. "Integration is the key to SAP." "Business reengineering is the key to SAP." "SAP is simpler than it appears to be; only the configuration is complex." Another of these phrases, repeated like a mantra throughout an SAP implementation, is:

AN SAP R/3 IMPLEMENTATION IS NOT A COMPUTER
PROJECT BUT A BUSINESS PROJECT

Cut this out and tape it your laptop screen. This phrase is repeated because the steps so commonly known for standard software projects do not apply for an SAP implementation. Methodologies for design and development of new systems or the implementation of best-of-breed software will include phases and tasks that are of no import to an SAP project. This phrase is true primarily because the emphasis of an SAP implementation is the **business** process re-design, not the design of the system that will support those processes.

To take it a step further:

AN SAP R/3 IMPLEMENTATION IS NOT A DIVISIONAL
COMPUTER PROJECT BUT AN ENTERPRISE-WIDE
BUSINESS PROJECT

Previous experience in IS projects can be more harmful than helpful if project members insist upon doing things as they have in the past. The following is a thumbnail sketch of the differences you will encounter.

Classical Software Project	SAP Project
Cater to individual divisions or departments	Address the company as a whole
Address incremental evolution	Force radical evolution
Software development is the primary activity (IS dominated)	Business reengineering is the primary activity (business dominated)
Project method is step by step and linear	Project method is iterative and interactive
IS and Users negotiate design	Users define usage

You will undoubtedly come across a variety of charts describing implementation steps, some of them the "wallpaper" box and quiver of arrows variety which list detail tasks over a three-year period. Some plans place more emphasis on SAP functionality than process redesign (or vice versa) while others focus on streamlining company processes. There is no single acceptable approach that must be adopted for an SAP implementation and anyone who tells you so is the kind of person who tells you there's only one car worth owning, only one beer worth drinking, and only one woman worth loving.

All the same, nearly all SAP implementations include the following elements or actions.

	ACTION	DECISION
	The Critical Event	SAP goes in; hell or high water
1	Envision the future	What will change?
2	Create Implementation Plan	Phased or Big Bang?
3	Form Your Team	Who will do what?
4	Install SAP	What pre-configuration?
5	Define SAP Hierarchies	Information architecture?
6	Redesign Processes	How will you work?
7	Configure SAP	How will it work for you?
8	Train Users	Who are the users?
9	System Migration	How to switch over?
10	Use the Systems	Monitor Benefits Realization

For the most part, these steps occur in a linear fashion, with some overlapping. The one point that will actually be addressed through all phases of the project is training.

The Critical Event

The CEO, or anyone else with real power (clout, the hammer), has the vision that SAP will be a cost cutting, streamlining, upgrading, inspiring, and evolutionary software platform to thrust your company into the next millennium. The word gets out. Confetti fills the air.

Envision the Future

This the first and most outlandish step in an SAP project. Dreaming isn't normally allowed in a business environment, but "that's how we do things 'round here" is an answer that will no longer suffice.

Now are you invited to imagine a company that works in the best possible fashion. This is the keynote phase to the reengineering process and this step should be approached as if you were starting the company over again.

This is not a tinkering phase or a time to simply fine-tune. You should be looking at your company from a fresh point of view, with a focus on:

- Why does your company do what it does?

- What are your strategic goals? Why have you considered implementing SAP?

- What changes will likely produce the most dramatic benefits?

- Where are the points of resistance to change and how can that resistance be eliminated?

Questions such as these should be asked at each level of the organization, in a descending fashion down the entire pyramid: company, sector, division, department, function. The current company structure should also be questioned, so that process redesign can occur on a diagonal, wall-busting plane. The SAP software that will support your new business processes is a diagonal application, meaning that it supports entire business processes that cross departmental boundaries and company hierarchies.

Let's go back to that phrase 'diagonal, wall-busting plane'. It sounds smooth, and will look smooth on a project plan, but the fact is that a diagonal, wall-busting plane is just what most people will resist because it not only affects the way they will be working, it may also affect them right out of their jobs or into new positions altogether. SAP implementations do not *require* this kind of re-structuring in all cases, but it can be an obvious result of serious business process reengineering intended to give both the company and SAP a chance to work some magic.

In a serious effort, the decision-making will be redistributed, and it is in this arena that you will find the highest level of resistance. Some staff will resent a loss of power and others will shy away from new responsibilities. The cultural changes will be surprising and, at least initially, bewildering.

It is not necessary to find the perfect plan for a perfect set of business processes. At this stage in the project, you should be working in headlines, with the smaller print of actual process redesign to occur later. If you start spinning your wheels at this juncture, the project will bog down.

Create an Implementation Plan

In establishing the scope of the project, you will be laying the groundwork toward answers to innumerable implementation questions that must be addressed in the plan. Scope factors include:

- How many sites, company entities, and users are envisioned?

- What legacy systems will be retained? Temporarily or permanently? What interfaces will be required?

- How vital is the elusive 20%? Must it be addressed in the first level of implementation? (The answer to this question is usually a firm 'No', but there will be more meetings over these issues than most project managers can bear.)

- What are the maximum benefits that can be obtained by using SAP? Whatever is required to realize these benefits should be at the center of the project scope.

The drafted implementation plan will address a major decision, the consequences of which cannot be overstated: how will you implement? In staged phases (often referred to as a rollout) or all at once, i.e. Big Bang? If only the answers were as simple as the phrases.

ROLLOUT	BIG BANG
Some functions can be implemented quickly	Implement only when all business units are ready
Tighter focus during initial system use	System use is widespread
Some integration is delayed	Integration is immediate
Temporary interfaces need to be written	No interfaces are needed
Medium risk	Medium to high risk

In a rollout implementation, individual functions or processes go live one or two at a time until all functions are fully implemented. Some rollouts are geographic based (site by site), others are domain based (finance first, then sales & distribution, then materials management, etc.), and others are necessity based, such as when some business units are ready to implement ahead of others. In a Big Bang implementation, all functions and processes go live at the same time. Whichever of these scenarios you choose, the resulting implementation plan must have milestones (or deadlines, if we have to use the word) which can be achieved and a project flow which can be measured on a daily basis.

For the purpose of brevity, we will not detail each of these task groups, which are, at any rate, self-evident. The time-line and project duration will vary depending upon the size of the company, number of users, implementation type, and number and type of applications being installed.

Form Your Team

Having developed the vision, you will now be in a position to form a team of individuals who can pursue that vision. For classical systems projects, this team would consist of a project manager, some systems analysts, user representatives, and an assortment of analyst and programming techies. IS top-heavy, in short. For an SAP project, the balance should be quite different.

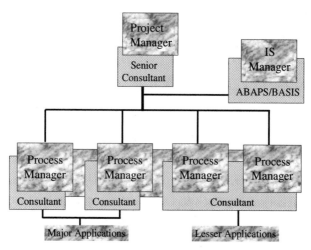

Consider the following staff chart:

Under this scheme, your staff is composed of process managers, each of whom is entrusted with responsibility for a specific application (or suite of applications). The process managers will master the functional aspects and have an understanding of the integration points for a module. In smaller companies (i.e. less than behemoth) it may be possible to have one person managing a suite of applications, such as SD through MM.

At the beginning of the project, each process manager would have a "shadow" consultant, either part-time or full time depending upon the scope. These consultants should bring their SAP experience and insight and the process managers should instigate the transfer of knowledge at the outset.

Note that these process managers should not be IS staff, but business staff from the departments relative to the applications. In addition to communication skills, clarity of thought, expertise in consensus building, a taste for change, boundless enthusiasm, a Mercedes laptop with all the gizmos, a dazzling wardrobe, fast car, and extreme patience, the process managers must also have *power*. They must be in a position to implement new business processes and practices, and to make decisions that will enable the company to use SAP as the enabler of those processes. If they are merely viewed as "coordinators", with little back-up from senior management, the exercise may resemble The University of (Insert Your Company Name), in which your company has been the subject of many term papers leading to no appreciable improvement.

Another point that must be clear as regards these people: they must have the time to devote to the project. Process managers should be assigned full-time and associated staff will inevitably have to be assigned at least half of their time or the project will definitely drift.

IS functions must be coordinated by an IS leader dedicated to the SAP project on a full-time basis. This individual should not have to toggle time between the SAP project and current systems. IS activities in the project may include some custom programming in ABAP/4 to fill functional gaps and, with shadow consulting available, your IS staff should be fully trained to BASIS and ABAP/4 programming.

At some point during the project, you should be able to lower the ratio of consulting time to in-house time. Remember that the aim is to use the consultants to provide knowledge and experience at the onset, and to transfer that knowledge and experience to your company.

At this point, a basic implementation plan should be established for the remaining phases of the project. After the next phase (installing SAP), the implementation plan can be fleshed out to task level. It is not advisable to attempt the creation of a highly detailed master plan prior to acquiring and installing SAP unless your team is also familiar with the pre-configured software you will be installing.

This is also a time when training should begin. This plan is not entirely linear, so you may want to jump ahead, briefly, to the section on training for some guidelines.

Install SAP ASAP

This certainly sounds easier than it seems because the installation process with SAP can take its own eternity. SAP provides only a fair amount of installation support, relying instead on its third party partners (i.e. platform  and/or consulting firms) to provide the help needed. That is why your team should already be in place.

To shorten and rationalize the inevitable configuring process, you should be looking toward installing a pre-configured "vanilla" system. By "vanilla", we mean a system configured generically enough so that the most common and frequent standard transactions are in place. By pre-configured, we mean that the basic configuration to be installed will fit the industry field in which you are working. In order to locate a pre-configured system, contact either SAP or the ICOE for your sector (more on this later). Failing that, find a company or two as similar to your own that are already using SAP and see if you can arrange something.

Do not install a basic, factory-packaged SAP if at all possible. Much of the subsequent configuration work would be unnecessarily complex and time-consuming. Invest your time searching for a configuration that someone else has puzzled over and carry on from there. The time spent investigating previously-accomplished configurations will pay off with a huge time savings in later implementation stages.

Define SAP Hierarchies

This can be the most painful part of an entire SAP process, because it strikes at the heart of how your company works. Companies with a high degree of vertical organization, in which various divisions have worked with great autonomy, find that SAP is "forcing" them to cross toward a more horizontal approach. Divisions that have been run as mini empires are difficult to bring into the SAP integrated scheme.

At issue is the hierarchy by which reporting, costing, and controls will be established. Some companies skirt this issue by running multiple SAP's for different business entities. These companies have invested megabucks for integrated systems and then decided to skip the integration, so let's assume that this isn't a recommended path. More enlightened companies struggle further with the hierarchy to take advantage of the horizontal approach to the reporting and data sharing concepts. At base, SAP seeks to create financial control across the spectrum, in which each business unit (division, group, office) can be viewed as a cost or profit center. What becomes a sticking point is that there is only *one* data base, no matter how many kingdoms have been established or how many presentation servers are installed.

The project cannot continue successfully until this hierarchy is firmly established and agreed upon. Thus, management holds the key. If the higher ups don't participate in the establishment of this hierarchy, resistance will perpetuate. Many an SAP implementation has foundered on just these rocks.

Some companies prefer creating an operational model or prototype once the project scope has been firmly established and new business processes have been mapped. The existence of a working model can pay huge dividends, including:

- A consequential, or parallel, gap analysis will occur and you will identify what functions or features SAP will not satisfy.

- "Proving" the desirability of implementing by offering a scale model of a working system (with defined processes) to people who are resisting the project.

- A first detailed view of your future workload will result and the project plan can be refined.

Sandboxing is a term that is sometimes used, and the image applies. What you are doing is building a sand castle. If it is not to your liking, you have only to knock it down and start again. The prototype can be changed throughout an iterative reengineering phase until an "ideal" model is agreed upon.

Before going on to business process reengineering, we feel compelled to add a firm note in regard to your gap analysis. A huge waste of time and money result when consultants or clients jump to hasty conclusions about what R/3 will or will not do for them. The easy reflex is to plan for add-on programming or, worse, the acquisition of other software that can be patched in to fulfill a function that R/3 ostensibly cannot satisfy.

The error is that at this point in the project, your staff certainly doesn't know enough about R/3 to make this call and your consultants may very well be in the same leaky boat. Therefore, let that gap analysis just simmer for a while. If you rush to address each identified gap, especially with 'inserted' new software, you will be losing much of what you purchased in the first place, namely the integration. Later in the project, when your knowledge of R/3 has deepened and widened, you will find that a number of those perceived gap issues will simply slide off the page. There *will* be functions and features that R/3 won't deliver, but you also have to ask yourself if the value of those functions outweighs the cost in time, money, and loss of R/3 integrity.

At this point in the project, you will need yet another tag taped to your laptop:

GAP ANALYSIS: THE ANALYSIS OF WHAT YOU WANT TO DO THAT YOU THINK WON'T BE PROVIDED BY SAP

Reengineer Business Processes

There is no way to relate, in a few words, all that you need to know about the reengineering of business processes. This is a subject that can require volumes to cover properly. We definitely recommend that anyone contemplating the acquisition and implementation of SAP should become versed in the principles and practice of process reengineering. Toward that end, we offer some of the basics.

1. Process reengineering is not the modifying or streamlining of existing business processes. Rather, it is the re-creation of business processes, at a fundamental level, with the purpose of radically improving the company in terms of its customer service or its economic posture, or both.

2. A business process is not an isolate element such as a task, an input, or an output. It is a suite of activities that culminate in output or a result that brings added value to the customer. An example is a process that begins with the receipt of an order from a customer, continues to the customer's receipt of goods, and ends with payment of those goods.

3. Be certain that the process managers will be given full responsibility for individual processes. It is they who have to sell new ideas to resistors and see the reengineering to its finish. These individuals will logically have sufficient clout and credibility within the organization; if not, even the most brilliantly conceived new processes may not be successfully implemented.

You begin with the assumption, generally true, that SAP offers the integrated functionality and system performance necessary to support the new organization that you've envisioned. Thus, at this point, you go about the detail of describing the great new business world that your company will become.

The descriptions can take many forms, but the most useful for an SAP implementation are visual depictions, such as process charts and data flow charts. SAP R/3 includes a working tool called the Analyzer, and although the user world is split on the advisability of using it, one can only wonder why the hesitation, if not for the fact that this tool is somewhat misunderstood. In the next section, the R/3 Reference Model is discussed. At this point in the project, the Analyzer could be used to chart existing business processes and, consequently, new and desired business processes.

For a raring-to-go company, charting current business processes may be only a huge waste of time. In essence, you'd be spending weeks or months documenting a business structure you intend to demolish. Better to carry on and start modeling the future.

However, a company struggling to come up with a vision for new business processes may find it instructive to chart existing processes with the Analyzer. Redundant activities and pointless processes would be rendered visible and the charts themselves will provide a shorthand tool for discussion.

Whichever way you decide to go, it is now essential that your business processes be fixed, not simply changed. Avoid the buzzwords and abstractions such as *empowerment, synergy, teaming,* et al and concentrate on cause and effect. Each new business process should have an identified trigger (a customer calls with an order) and an identified consequence, or series of consequences (the order is entered into the system, a confirmation issued, and a stock request sent). In turn, a given consequence will be a trigger in another process.

What you are searching for is workflow, an acceleration of business processes through the elimination of unnecessary worker intervention or system dead ends. You are also searching for automated connections to both clients and suppliers (think Electronic Data Interchange).

Failures will occur, and should not be punishable by death. Each radical change carries risk, and these risks should be measured against anticipated benefits.

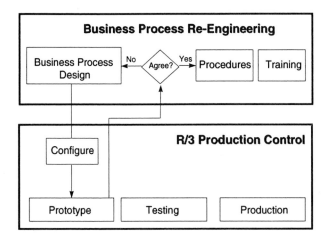

BPR and R/3 configuration lie squarely on the critical path of an R/3 implementation, and these two activities are linked and iterative. Repeat, iterative. This is the point at which too many methodologies, linear in scope, bog down. An R/3 implementation is a series of bubbles that have to be burst, curlicues, not straight lines. Configuration logically follows BPR, and in many cases, configuration failures lead to new BPR or new items in the gap analysis that may have to be addressed with ABAP/4 add-ons. Some companies are tempted to accelerate the process by leaving configuration to the consultants while speeding ahead with BPR. This is not advisable. Your staff should be taking the lead in the configuring process so that once the consultants are gone, you will find yourselves firmly at the wheel.

Our friend and colleague, Jim O'Keefe, likens R/3 to an erector set, his principle being that you have all the pieces you need to build whatever you want and as long as you don't bend the pieces (i.e. modify the base code), you can re-build what you will later want with the same pieces. The configuring process is therefore comparable to choosing your pieces and settling how they will fit together. It is what happens with an R/3 implementation, this fitting together of parts. BPR only provides part of what you will need. Familiarity with SAP R/3 is the other essential.

Configure SAP

In the four years since R/3 was introduced, the perception (and sometimes painful reality) has been that SAP takes an eternity to implement. When interviewed, people complain about two aspects in particular: reengineering (which is their turf) and configuring (which is SAP's). The configuration is the process by which functions are tailored to your requirements: screen layouts and masking, data flows, the rules of processing, etc.

There are literally thousands of configuration options and sorting through them to fit the system to your business processes can be mind-numbing and time-consuming. This is the other edge of the SAP broadsword. There is quite simply so much functionality and flexibility built into the system that mere mortals can't keep up.

To this point, you have the "vanilla-preconfigured" version and a new and detailed configuring map based upon your new business process designs. It is not an obligation to complete the configuration to the last detail before implementing. This is where so very many implementations hit the skids and the whirlwind of design-configure-design-configure turns SAP projects into three-way mudwrestling matches between implementers, users, and the system itself.

Our earnest advice is to seek a cut-off point at which individual and detail requirements be set aside and system migration be allowed to commence. Once SAP is in production, the configuration process can go on.

Addressing this daunting facet of its existence, SAP has come up with a variety of solutions and tools:

The R/3 Reference Models

With this tool, you can create and modify the components and flow of various business processes (referred to as "event-driven process chains" or EPC's) within the system. This considerably eases confusion, since the EPCs 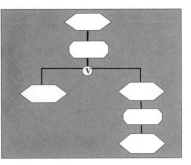 are depicted in simple and clear flow charts of events (i.e. the customer calls in a sales order) and functions (sales order entry) and the configuring process is not simply a series of codes and switches.

Once the Reference Model is satisfactory, you can use the R/3 Procedure Model which describes all of the tasks involved in an implementation, including the dependencies between project stages and work steps, standard settings, and recommendations. The Reference Model will serve as a companion to the Procedure Model; between these two, the documentation, on-line help, training materials, data models, and process models are integrated.

In all, the Reference Model allows for system depiction at five levels. In addition to process view, are:

- Information flow, describing the relationships and attributes between senders and receivers of information.

- Data models showing data entities that are key to company activities (as depicted in the process flows). Though different data levels can be viewed, only the first level of detail is required for business definitions.

- Function viewing will show a snapshot/chart of the company's defined hierarchy. This is a static view, changed only according to the hierarchical definition.

- Organization, in which certain organizational relationships are delineated.

R/3 Pre-Set Configurations

Given the large number of R/3 installations in existence, the live configurations of R/3 are multiplying. SAP has been gathering a library of diverse configuration sets for some time and customers are invited to take any of these and apply them directly if so desired.

If you use the SAP customizing tools or take a pre-set configuration, you can drastically reduce the implementation time and get your company up and running on SAP. Despite the continual complaints about lengthy implementations, dozens of companies have implemented all or part of SAP in mere months. The reasons for success vary, but one constant has been management determination in the realm of configuring the system to meet the defined business processes and not getting stuck in office politics, power struggles, and the like. Companies that are taking an eternity to implement SAP should, in many cases, stop harping about the configuration logjam and focus instead upon the preceding business process issues.

Train Your Staff

Training is an ongoing concern throughout the duration of an SAP implementation, and it is one of the thornier issues in an SAP project. Training resources are varied and finding adequate training (the right course for the right individual at the right time) is not a simple task.

There are three levels of training to be addressed:

1. management training

2. implementation team training

3. user training.

First, a note about consultants and *their* training. In reaction to the great demand for qualified SAP consultants, too many consulting firms have thrown bodies into mass "academy" training courses offering function by function overviews, a bit of ABAP/4, a seminar on the integration of functions, another four days on configuration, and very little individual Q&A. Certificates are issued and the phrase "SAP Certified" comes into play.

'Certified' is not the same as qualified. We even know of one engagement manager who judges new employees by their performance at one of these academies. The certification exam is so simple that if they can't pass it, they are soon transferred or terminated. Be slow to embrace consultants with only this certification to offer as evidence of their SAP worth.

For the implementation team, SAP client training can be arranged through the SAP offices throughout the country. This training can be made to focus on specific functions (Sales & Distribution, Production Planning, et al). Unfortunately, the people who provide this training are often professional trainers, not people with actual SAP flight logs.

Industry Centers of Expertise were instituted in 1995 to act as liaison between SAP and customers in various sectors. Typical of SAP, they are referred to as ICOEs but that's more initials-identity obsession. These centers provide assistance in finding configuration sets and providing working models to fit individual company needs, and are divided into:

Automotive	Consumer Packaged Goods
Healthcare	Financial Service Industry
Oil and Gas	High Tech/Electronics
Process Industries	Utilities & Communications

Operation Jumpstart commenced in May of 1994. It consists of an overview class for all team members, and then special sessions for specific fields of interest (SD, FI, what have you). Initially, these courses were available every two weeks in Atlanta, Chicago, Foster City, Philadelphia, and Toronto, and new sites have been added, including Boston, Dallas, Calgary, Montreal, Cleveland, Cincinnati, St. Louis, Minneapolis, and Irvine, CA. More are sure to be added. Check with your SAP rep for the site closest to you, but remember, these classes are what they say they are, a jump-start. Further training will be required, and at various levels for various team members.

Project managers should master system architecture (particularly as it pertains to the hierarchy), tools (ARIS,

Navigator, et al for customizing and reengineering), and the ins and outs of configuring.

Process managers should seek training at the SAP centers for the areas in which they will be responsible.

Company management should receive considerable overview and training to SAP as well, even though fulltime project involvement may not be planned. Think of top management as the 'owners' of business processes. Final decisions relative to re-engineering will be theirs, so a familiarity with SAP on an organizational level will be needed.

Later on in the project, user training will occur. By user training, we mean the training of those people who will actually be touching the system on a daily basis. In order to eliminate dependence upon SAP and/or those pricey consultants, you should consider establishing a three-generational scheme for initial training: A consultant teaches your manager all about a function. The manager teaches the users. One user is assigned as ongoing internal training consultant. There are other variants, including the notion of including Super Users within the configuring team. Either approach is viable. Flip of a coin.

Throughout the life cycle of the system, on-line help and on-line documentation are available, but these features are not always as helpful as you'd like, and nothing can replace one-on-one tutoring.

What is important is that your own staff master the functions as soon as possible and as completely as possible, so that you will not be dependent upon consultants for the ongoing use of the system. Again, the **transfer of knowledge** is the key here (that's why it's always in bold).

In summary, training options include:

- SAP-specific training companies (refer to the last pages of this book)

- Industry Centers of Expertise

- SAP training through SAP America (individual course offerings are throughout the year)

- Consultant training, if truly qualified consultants can be found

- Send an employee to a company already using SAP for training

- Intensive use of on-line documentation and on-line help.

System Migration

Whichever implementation route you've chosen, rollout or Big Bang, each of the business modules will now migrate from legacy systems to SAP. The order in which this migration occurs is up to company needs and strategy, but logical system segments should be migrated together if integration is an issue. For example, all applications relative to order fulfillment (SD and probably MM and maybe PP) may need to be migrated at the same time. Human Resources (HR) might best be implemented first in order to facilitate eventual workflow.

Have we already made it clear that we view interfacing as an evil that should be avoided wherever possible? If the implementation is the rollout variety, interfaces cannot be avoided, since links between SAP and legacy systems will be required. As final implementation nears, some departments of your company will be more prepared than others and the temptation to settle on interfaces (temporarily, of course) will be strong. Avoid this temptation. Interfacing to SAP is complex and time-consuming and the more of it you do, the longer you put off final implementation.

It may be better to live with a number of *manual* processes for a determined period than to undertake an elaborate interfacing subproject. Legacy systems that are not destined for the scrap heap will require interfacing. Nothing's perfect in life. Go ahead.

Know When You're Finished and Say So

If you have followed a well-constructed implementation plan, knowing the point at which it has been fulfilled will be relatively easy. SAP R/3 will be running in most of your divisions, output will be flowing, and the company will have already begun to reap the anticipated benefits. You should be prepared to invoke the 80 percent rule, having reached critical mass. Your business is running and that other twenty percent will be a daily, constant shifting target, so if the transfer of knowledge has been successful, boot out those consultants and get on with your business.

We don't mean to dictate your behavior at this or at any point in the project, but at this point, please, let everyone know that you have reached the end. Make it a celebration, not just another day at the racetrack. Obviously, there will be kinks to work out, processes to be reconsidered, software to be patched in, but this will always be the case. Having SAP up and running doesn't qualify everyone for early retirement, except the consultants if you haven't yet thanked them, toasted them, and politely shown them the door.

Internal staff that has been assigned full time to the SAP project can now ride off into the sunset and resume their former lives, though some will prefer to continue with SAP in some capacity, while others will be headhunted right out of your company and into consulting if their efforts (and newly-acquired SAP expertise) aren't recognized.

Post implementation tactics will vary depending upon the level of success of the implementation. Now is the time to return to those intentions and visions of the first step and measure how closely you have come to achieving them. It is also a time for a new vision, a return to the beginning of the system life cycle, but this time rippling with SAP muscle.

A New Vision of the System Life Cycle

The life cycle of an information system has traditionally been viewed as circular:

- the perception of a need

- planning

- acquisition/development

- implementation and utilization

- degradation = the growing perception of a need.

Once SAP is implemented, the system may no longer follow this pattern. Add-on modules and upgrades may always be needed, as well as that elusive twenty percent. But for the core of your business (and a large core at that) you should not find it necessary to redesign or replace software. As needs arise and the performance of the system is found wanting, your company may find it advantageous to re-engineer business processes and reflect changes in the SAP configuration.

:
:
:

History of an SAP Implementation

A Case Study

A Question of Propriety

Every software implementation project has a history that is
usually told in a variety of ways: project documentation, a file
of memos to and from, coffee room chatter. What tends to
happen is that the history is of huge import to one and all
during the implementation, and then all is usually forgotten
once the system is up and running.

This is not the case for SAP implementations, for which war
stories abound, and companies considering joining the SAP
implementation band wagon search high and low for truths that
case studies may tell. Some cases studies are cautionary tales,
others are merely meant to be instructive. None are dull.

The case study that follows is real, but for proprietary reasons,
the company identity will not be revealed. This is not a case of
'the names are changed to protect the innocent.' Rather, the
inner workings of the company should not be laid out, at least
at this time, for all the world to see. However, the activities that
are detailed in this case study are accurately depicted.

The Critical Event

A company in the business of manufacturing, marketing, and sales of finished wood products, employing more than 1200 people across four sites, with an annual turnover of $1.5B and assets in excess of $750M, found itself in a huge dilemma. For five years running, the company had not been generating a satisfactory return on investment. The share price on the stock market had been in constant decline for two years, and the company had begun receiving an unfavorable credit rating from S&P and Moody. Given this kind of performance, both cashflow and the cost of borrowing money were of major concern to the company.

Obviously, senior management was doing everything to turn the company around, but reliable and timely information was not provided by its information systems. In terms of financial data, the systems were close to useless.

The company purchased its raw material -lumber- from both domestic and foreign markets. As such, financial officers needed information vital for hedging foreign purchases. They needed real time costing data, an accurate inventory position for raw materials, semi-finished, and finished products, production planning, maintenance planning, general ledger, accounts payable and accounts receivable.

Current systems were linked by interfaces across applications and sites and these interfaces were slow, with costly time lags. Manual reconciliations of data could not be made fast enough. Worse, despite the presence of an army of systems analysts for maintenance of these systems, the interfaces were breaking down on a weekly basis.

The Chief Operations Officer of the company, enormously frustrated with the situation, was given the mission of turning the financial picture around. Various attempts to improve data systems had already failed, and a new vision was called for. The vision that was established, the gauntlet, as it were, was two-fold:

1. The company initiated a project to reengineer business processes with the help of a Big 6 consulting firm.

2. The company began the searched for an integrated software suite running on a state-of-the-art technology platform to replace their legacy systems.

Given a scant budget, and using primarily in-house resources, the company underwent what it thought to be a reengineering of business processes, but what was in reality a simple-minded and radical downsizing  of staff. Few new procedures were introduced and no dramatic changes were made to their way of doing business. They were doing what they had always done, albeit with fewer people.

In parallel, the company considered over thirty different software alternatives, then pared the list down to three. Of the three finalists, only SAP offered real time updating on an integrated scale. It seemed to management the only choice.

Reality Bites: Initial Mistakes Lead to a Re-Start

Given the serious straits the company found itself in, an initial implementation budget of $7.5M was established. Very little consulting was called for, and none of it at project management level. At this point, management assumed that its prior 'reengineering' project had put the company in a position for a smooth implementation of SAP software.

Only a few short months later, as project employees began to understand how little they really knew about SAP, an additional $3M was requested, bringing the budget to $10.5M. At the same time, the few consultants who'd been brought in were found to be lacking in true and tested SAP experience.

The multiplicity of sites, coupled with a lack of project management, led to a failure in process re-design. Employees from diverse sites were going in different directions and turf battles reigned. Something had to give, and well before that first $10.5M had been thrown down the tubes, upper management suspended the project, took a look down the road, and came up with three alternatives:

1. scrap the project entirely, which would have left them still in the dark and still losing money

2. continue with the project as it was going, but tighten up the coordination between sites

3. start over with the help of experienced project management.

Swallowing hard, but more determined than ever, upper management chose the third option. A new budget was drawn up, calling for $18M, and this time including a project manager and as many as fifteen outside consultants. The number of consultants budgeted had more to do with budget constraints than with a clear vision of consulting requirements. And at this point, the roles of consultants had not been addressed. The feeling was: Get help. Now.

Having failed once, upper management felt that the key would be to find a good project manager. Candidates from rival Big 6 firms and the platform partner were interviewed, but the job was entrusted to a project manager from OR Partner (a member of the Consulting Alliance), a man with five years of SAP experience (battle scars, that grizzled veteran gaze). Call him Daniel.

On taking the job, Daniel and management agreed on two points. First, that he be viewed by all employees as a member of the company, not some outside mercenary. Upper management entrusted him to do all he could to bring in the project under budget and on time, and would not be second-guessing him in this regard. Secondly, Daniel would have authority over critical decisions and continual upper management presence on the project.

One keynote in the relationship between Daniel and senior staff was his belief that twelve consultants, rather than fifteen, should be required to complete the job. Whereas other consultants had suggested sending far in excess of this number to the project, Daniel was already squeezing the budget to its core.

As will be seen, the element of trust and cooperation between the project manager and the company's senior staff was one of the key factors in the ultimate project success. Instant budget trimming was a plus in Daniel's favor, maybe a personal coup. As will be seen, he was able to back up his power play.

Impressed by Daniel's budget mastery, senior executives also agreed to adopt the project method that Daniel suggested.

Project Initiation	Conceptual Design	Detailed Design

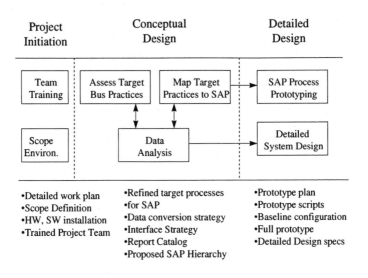

- •Detailed work plan
- •Scope Definition
- •HW, SW installation
- •Trained Project Team

- •Refined target processes
- •for SAP
- •Data conversion strategy
- •Interface Strategy
- •Report Catalog
- •Proposed SAP Hierarchy

- •Prototype plan
- •Prototype scripts
- •Baseline configuration
- •Full prototype
- •Detailed Design specs

System Development & Testing	System Cutover & Rollout

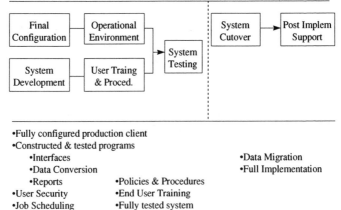

- •Fully configured production client
- •Constructed & tested programs
    - •Interfaces
    - •Data Conversion
    - •Reports
- •User Security
- •Job Scheduling

- •Policies & Procedures
- •End User Training
- •Fully tested system

- •Data Migration
- •Full Implementation

Project Initialization

High Level Strategy

Project objectives had already been established and were re-iterated as:

- improvement of profitability
- improved productivity and efficiency
- reduction of operational costs
- an elevation of company morale.

The existence of real time decisional data on an integrated data base was seen as paramount to the company. In addition, a successful project was needed to improve company morale, obviously somewhat low in the wake of the preceding "downsizing" and initial project failure.

Anticipated Benefits

Upper management anticipated annual hard dollar savings of $15 to $25M based upon anticipated net profit gains through the availability of real time price and costing data.

Additional 'soft dollar' benefits anticipated were:

- staff reduction (unmeasured at this point)
- middle to long term reduction of systems costs
- marketing/purchasing improvements
- integrated storehouse
- inventory management.

Launch of Change Management Effort

Taking the reins as project manager, Daniel recommended to upper management that communication to employees be loud and clear to avoid paranoiac reactions in regard to a further downsizing and to provide employees some understanding of the true purposes and goals of the project. Activities which were planned and carried out included:

1. a brown paper bag meeting - over a six-week period, management visited the various sites and presented the project outline, taking time to answer questions in a town hall format;

2. a document describing project goals, content, duration, etc. was distributed to all employees;

3. a project newsletter was established on a monthly basis to update employees on the status of the project.

Throughout the project, this move proved to have been the right one. Negative reactions to the project, which were obvious during the first attempt, were considerably lessened. One hurdle (lack of upper management participation) was cleared early on, setting the stage for middle management participation.

Implementation Plan

A modified version of the Big Bang implementation method was planned in which basic Finance, Sales & Distribution (SD), and Materials Management (MM) would be implemented across all sites in a first phase, with Controlling (CO) and Assets Management (AM) implemented across all sites in second phase, and the remainder of Financials implemented across all sites in a final phase.

Phase	Applications	Duration	Timescale
1	SD, MM, Basic FI	12 months	12 months
2	CO, AM	6 months	18 months
3	PM,PP,HR, All of FI	12 months	30 months

In essence, one Big Bang followed by one littler bang and another Big Bang. The deadlines were imposed by the company's urgent need to install the Financials quickly in order to survive. It was understood that some quality corners would be cut in terms of business procedures, but the first phase was to plug the information gap in order to turn the company into a profit situation.

The deadline was also strict because of flagging company morale. Pay rises had been suspended and workloads were high due to the downsizing. There was some doubt as to how long management could use the whip on its tired horses.

Team Formation: Addition By Subtraction

Although the budget called for more consultants, Daniel configured a staff with only twelve for the first phase. Four were assigned to Financials (FI), three to Sales & Distribution SD), three to Materials Management (MM) and the remaining two were assigned primarily to Basis.

The over-all project hierarchy was established as follows:

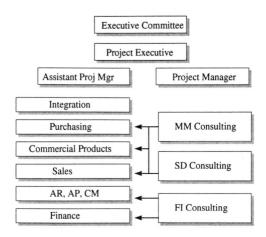

At the formation of this team, two objectives were established, the first being the obvious objective of implementing SAP and the second being the need for the client to be self-sufficient in SAP terms by the project's conclusion. The client would inevitably needs its own project manager and a reduced consultant staff. To meet this second objective, a program for a transfer of knowledge was instituted and fulfilled throughout the project.

For each phase and sub-phase of the project, client staff was tutored in the meaning behind each task as well as task content. Client staff then fulfilled initial tasks of each subphase with the collaboration of consultants, with their results being monitored by both the 'shadow' consultant and the project manager. This was an iterative process, with client staff mastering SAP tasks such as configuring over a period of time. As the project progressed, the shadow consultants transferred more and more to the client project staff, who were by this time receiving their directions directly from the project manager and the assistant project manager.

At the beginning of the project, Daniel developed a high level plan, which was reviewed by the executive committee, and a detailed plan, which was reviewed by the project executive and the project team leaders. The high level plan was generally distributed, rather than the detail plan in order to let client staff learn the methodology by following stage by stage, without being overwhelmed at the beginning. From phase to phase, detail plans were distributed and explained.

Daniel knew that the client staff assigned to the project would be undergoing career transformations once the transfer of knowledge from himself and his consulting team took place. Thus, he informed client management that they should prepare for nearly a 30% loss of staff assigned to the project. Given the popularity of SAP in North America and the concurrent shortage of experienced consultants, many project members would resign to go into the lucrative consulting business.

In reaction, management determined that each client staff member assigned to the project should have a back-up, so that a second level of knowledge transfer would occur. Happily, this back-up took place, as the client began to lose staff eight months after the project began and continually thereafter. Management had considered finding ways to retain staff through raises, bonuses, and promotions, but realized that back-ups would be in the same gravy boat. Thus, it was decided to simply swallow whatever losses occurred and carry on. The reduction of client staff had some impact on the quality of the project in some areas, but because of the survival dictum, the deadline for phase one was not delayed.

Another key decision made early on in the project was the location for project activities. The struggle in the first go-round had been between the western city where financial operations were centered and an eastern city where operations and materials were located.

When Project Management, not the Implementation, is the Battleground

Since SAP relies on both consulting and platform partners to assist in implementations, the position of project manager is of key interest. It is, after all, the project manager who is directly responsible for the day-to-day and over-all project operations, and it is the project manager who has the greatest say-so when it comes to staffing (and, sigh, billing) from the outside. Thus, the struggle between outside consulting and platform companies to place their own project manager can be fierce.

In this case, Daniel had to suffer second-guessing and continual carping from one of the other partners which had initially offered the client its own project manager and was rebuffed. When the client defended Daniel and it was clear that the partner couldn't have him removed as project manager, they made him a job offer, which he turned down. It was only after a number of months that Daniel was fully able to simply do his job for the client. This scenario is, sadly, not uncommon in the world of SAP implementations.

What must be remembered: from wherever he or she comes, the project manager has to work entirely for the client, without outside pressures in regard to consultant staffing levels or consulting sources.

Daniel chose to set up project operations in the western city and thus eastern staff was obliged to travel there in order to work on the project. This may have seemed a hindrance at first, but by getting eastern staff offsite, Daniel was able to get them to concentrate on SAP rather than their previous positions. Some of the clear advantages of moving a team offsite during business process reengineering are:

- staff isn't swamped by current day-to-day activities; new ideas can be generated more freely and with greater concentration

- having all of the staff in the same location for key periods of time allows for a clearer vision of the integration points between applications

- keeping consultants close to client project staff helps avoid both project drifting and scope creep (the almost invisible widening of project scope that occurs when staff elements are distant).

The detailed work plan, to task level, was created on Microsoft Project, and was based upon the SAP R/3 implementation methodology detailed earlier. Some considerations in the detailed work were:

- Cost accounting by task wasn't an issue; the key cost to be monitored was the outside consulting cost of 12 consultants at rate for 24 months; in essence, holding that line. Planned and actual project status were followed on a GANTT chart on a weekly basis.

- Internal project staff were added on as a project cost (and therefore part of the capital investment, overall).

- Team leaders tracked time spent and reported base estimates rather than hours to the project manager.

Installation of SAP Software

In order to allow for an orderly progression of events, three "instances" of SAP were installed, with a total of six "clients" or versions. It should be noted that a company can install any number of 'instances' or 'clients', being limited only by system capacity and memory. (Note: as of this printing, SAP standard licensing allows for three instances. Any more instances require additional licensing.)

Daniel knew that control of the quality from step to step would be a huge issue in such a rapid project, and thus had SAP installed according to this scheme.

Instance 1	Instance 2	Instance 3
Sandbox	Quality Assurance	Production
Proto & Development	Training	
Testing		

Sandbox was used for what you might imagine, playing with tables and transactions, trial and error prototyping and configuring, etc.

Prototyping & Development was used for actual prototyping and thus better controls were required for the generation of test data and the changing of table settings.

Testing was an even more refined and controlled instance, in which no deletions or changes could be made without the approval of the Process Owner and Team Leader.

Quality Assurance was the pre-production version, with fully controlled and pre-defined access. This version was used for integrated testing and stress testing, and contained only high quality master data.

Training was pretty much a copy of the Quality Assurance version, in which development or table changes was forbidden.

Production was the final live system.

This compartmentalization of various versions would allow for system development controls and software integrity. Once this series of instances was established, conceptual design began with vigor.

Conceptual Design

Concurrent Scope & Strategy   for Business Process Redesign

From the outset, it was evident that the client had too many isolated processes and little integration. Communication and data interchanges were largely vertical and had to be radically broken down into more horizontal directions.

Contrary to other projects, there was little overt resistance to sometimes sweeping changes in business processes. Daniel observed that this was due to a number of factors, primarily:

- Ideas were sold to executives first, then at the lower levels (top of each vertical slot) looking for the buying-into of the concept.

- The changes were unanimously accepted by executive council.

- The company was in a survival mode and there was no time for nit-picking about details.

One example of a radical change in company thinking was in the realm of purchasing. Prior to this project, the purchases of wood/lumber futures were seen as isolated and different from regular purchases of materials. Traditionally, there had been separate sub-systems for each type of purchase. Daniel convinced management that this distinction wasn't necessary. In his words, "you buy, you buy; you sell, you sell." Thus, incorporating a one buy (purchase) and one sell (of futures) process into the mainstream of purchasing procedures was facilitated, albeit with a separate set of procedures, rules, and controls for each type of purchase.

Conceptual Design

Steps for conceptual design were somewhat classic to an SAP project.

AS IS - scripting of current business processes in a step-by-step format. Otherwise known as the Consulting Director's Retirement Fund Phase. Happily, in this case, cut to the proper bone.

TO BE Process Flow Diagrams. The team used Visio for this output. The Analyzer was not available at the onset of the project and once it was available, there was no compelling reason to change tools.

TO BE Process Mapping. This was a more detailed inventory of steps within processes.

TO BE Script List. This was a list and detail of functional requirements leading toward the configuration of SAP.

Each of these tasks were performed by client project staff, with the assistance and guidance of the consulting staff. Process owners had to approve each of the TO BE documents. Disputes regarding new processes were filtered to the project manager and, where necessary, to the Project Executive for deliberation and final decisions.

Given the survival deadline, no add-on development or modification was called for in the project plan. All attention to niceties was postponed until after the initial implementation. It is fascinating to note that in such a project environment, the absence of sideline, non-critical issues was actually of benefit. Strict business issues were directly addressed, without the usual arguments about the need for add-on developments. What was on order was SAP and no cheese or bacon or lettuce, thank you.

Detail Design

With a completed conceptual design, project staff was able to turn to the mind-boggling step of configuring SAP to meet that conceptual design.

Four sides of design were addressed:

1. Business Processes
2. Data conversion
3. Interfaces
4. Reports.

Data conversion was a relatively straightforward design, using one-time interfaces for the large master files or manual entry for other, smaller, files.

A special task force of client staff was formed to study requirements for management reporting, with the charge to study all reporting aspects of SAP such as ABAP Query or online display, not only EIS functions. Inevitably, an EIS was built, but reporting for middle management was also prepared at this stage.

Beyond the business process scripts, the configuring teams needed to focus on the business practices and procedures governing each process.

Daniel was convinced that more than any of the sub-phases involved in an SAP project, this was usually the most important and the most neglected. The value of procedural rules and data validations to the final integrity of the system data is enormous. This step is often neglected because, quite frankly, wading through the rules and procedures can be quite a pain in the ass. It is a task of details, and more often than not, the people in charge of business processes don't have the least idea what the processing rules, authorities, or data validations should be. In the case of Daniel's project, some procedures proved to be outdated, while others were unclear or not enforced. Thus, detail digging and concentration were required during this step in the detail design.

Since SAP software is shared across the company, there can only be one version of that software. As such, company-wide rules and procedures had to be established and, where possible, enforced by the system. What if the user doesn't want to issue a requisition prior to a purchase order? Under what conditions can this be done? With what authorities? What products can be sold for prices other than those listed in pricing master files? Who has the authority to amend pricing?

Answers to these questions feed directly into the configuring process (mandatory fields, authorities, exceptions processing, etc.) If enough questions are answered prior to turning to configuration, the task will be vastly simplified. As it happens, some of these issues still had to be neglected in the first phase because of the survival deadline. Further, some of the business team leaders failed to provide a detailed version of their business practices. This failure led to more simplified (and less stringent) system controls. Additional configuring was required after completion of the first phase.

System Development & Testing

Final SAP Configuration

Actual configuration was performed by individual teams with a mix of:

consultants (to guide) + client team (to do) + IS staff (to support)

In many projects, IS staff is not a part of the configuring process, but at this client, a portion of the IS staff was being converted away from classic IS functions and into more business-oriented positions. Therefore, their involvement in configuring was desirable.

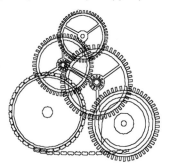

It was during the configuring process that the organization of the various installed versions of SAP came into play. Configuring sub-teams were working in the somewhat controlled environment of the Prototype version and only final configurations were then passed on to the Testing version. In actuality, configurations were manually re-created in the Testing version only after Process Owners and Team Leaders were in agreement.

In the subsequent testing sub-phase, if results were not satisfactory, design changes had to be made in the Prototype/Development version, re-approved, and carried back to Testing all over again.

The basis of the configuring process were the scripts and maps created in the previous phase, which, by their format, tended to offer a measurement of many of the anticipated benefits by a simple contrast between AS IS and TO BE.

Old Hats, New Hats, What's a Hat?

There's an old Steve Martin routine in which he talks about how those crazy French have a different word for everything. For example, he says, taking off his hat, in France, this isn't a hat, it's a *chapeau!*

While attempting to implement SAP, Daniel and his team found that the client had developed dissimilar materials master files at the various sites, and there would be a nightmare reconciling not only at the material code level, but also within each record for the short description.

One flagrant example of a disfigured file was the simple hard hat. *Casque rigide* to the French, Steve. Not only was the same article given different codes, it was also variously described as a hard hat, protective headgear, safety cap, construction headgear, et al. Small wonder that they didn't find one instance of 'industrial work person's cranial protection unit'.

In some cases, new standards had to be developed and applied for the materials master. In other cases, vendor descriptions and sometimes codes were used, which greatly facilitated purchasing by eliminating vendor-client confusion as to what was ordered.

Another difficulty encountered by the team was that SAP does not allow for negative inventory. This was troublesome in terms of the manner in which wood products raw materials buying and selling is conducted. There is a gap of time during which a product may already have been sold in excess of inventory (while a concurrent purchase of the raw materials needed for manufacturing is in progress) and the 'deal' is only closed when the balance of that material is 'delivered'. Quantities of delivered wood do not have to be exactly as ordered. Exact amounts delivered are not known until actual delivery has taken place.

If the system allowed for negative inventory, this process would have been seamless. As it stands, some deals cannot be closed until inventory is positive, thus causing a delay to those deals.

When the configuration process was completed, the Test version was loaded to the Quality Assurance instance for final integration and stress testing.

System Development

As previously stated, no add-on development was called for in this first phase of the project due to time and budget constraints, Thus, system development was limited to:

- Preparations and guidelines for manual builds of vendor and client master files. The manual approach was adopted because of the relatively low volume of conversions to be done and the disparities between legacy systems and new SAP master file content.

- External interface (to banks for Electronic Financial Transfers and to suppliers with Electronic Data Interchange)

- Permanent internal interfaces to legacy systems that would continue after the SAP implementation

- Data conversion interfaces for the higher volume materials files.

Operational Environment Set Up

A total of over 500 authorized users were planned for the system. The hardware platform included the base system, a Database Server, and a Development Server, and two desktop Application Servers.

System access was handled by Token Ring for all users and the Windows environment was chosen for screen display and Microsoft Office capacity.

Volume studies and transaction measurements were made for each of the modules being implemented, and well before this phase began, all equipment was in place and tested.

User Training & Procedures

Concurrent to the operational environment set up, user training and procedures began in earnest. Prior to this point, a base user orientation had already occurred. Because the Windows standard had been chosen and client staff was not up to par for this, a special training coordinator was given the task of training client staff to Windows and Microsoft Office. This became a permanent position in the company, as it became obvious that ongoing support beyond the project was needed.

At this point, the project team was split into two distinct groups. Half of the team was assigned to integrated tests and the other half to continue to develop user procedures and monitor user training.

Because of budget limitations, no external consulting was employed for user training and no extra documentation was purchased.

Instead, client project staff performed user training with scripts made during detail design as a basis for a) establishing how the system was to be used and b) for the completion of procedures writing.

A minor amount of customizing was required to convert scripts to final procedures. Once this was accomplished, full user training commenced, including the following steps:

1. Super users were identified for each business sector
2. Super users were trained by client staff
3. Super users were involved in the integrated system test
4. Super users trained other users in their sectors

For the longer term, super users were given the responsibility of ongoing onsite support.

System Testing

As previously mentioned, unit tests were accomplished during the configuration process.With a configured system now resident in the Quality Assurance version, this is where integration testing was accomplished.

Full system testing and cycle testing were completed, with the timing intended to dovetail with the completion of user training. This was due to the wish to allow users to come fresh from training (rather than allow a lag) so that they could complete the final testing phase, user acceptance testing.

System Cutover & Rollout

The initial plan was for a parallel run of SAP and legacy systems for a period of two months, during which process and team leaders would monitor results and, if they were satisfactory, the project executive, project manager, and relevant process owner would sign the OK to drop legacy systems being replaced by SAP.

For the most part, the parallel run was smooth. User training proved to be sufficient in terms of operations, but the legacy systems were still being relied upon far too much for reporting purposes. The cultural change was taking its sweet time, and this was the one major unforeseen problem. Data needed for reporting was slow in coming from some sources and the users balked, feeling a need to carry on longer with legacy systems. A third parallel month was agreed upon, during which the process owners in the slow sector were engaged in attacking the delay problems.

At the end of three months, SAP was running as planned for FI, SD, and MM. Though two more phases of cutover were left to be accomplished, critical mass had been reached and the company was firmly on its SAP path.

Soul Searching

In over-all terms, the project has to be viewed as successful in that SAP was implemented within the imposed time-frame and the client is now reaping the benefits that were envisioned. Operations have been streamlined and both delivery turnaround and information turnaround have been vastly reduced. Moreover, the bottom line has taken a major turn for the better and the survival of the company is no longer a daily worry.

Looking back, three key elements contributed to project success:

1. the company's need to survive, coupled with the previous failure to implement, lent impetus to all project activities;

2. upper management took an active role in the project and clearly communicated its commitment to company employees;

3. the mix of consulting and client staff was reasonable and the accent on transfer of SAP knowledge was successful.

All the same, in looking back over the duration of the project, a number of ways in which it might have been more successful come to light.

At the heart of the project, initial missteps were costly for too many months into the project. The partnering process was flawed and should have been mastered earlier on, particularly as concerns the project management.

Secondly, after the initial implementation failure, the client was understandably but incorrectly impatient to see progress in the second attempt. Project initialization was therefore rushed, and much of the project method and organization had to be established on the run instead of at the onset. Another month, or even two, may not have had a serious impact upon the company in terms of its financial position, but would have allowed the project team to plan the project with more expertise and less haste. It is certain that the business process redesign and the accompanying rules and procedures would have been of a higher quality and far more comprehensive than those that were used during the first months after implementation.

A third change that the project manager would make would be to institute a master data management practice at the beginning of the project. Master data was neglected throughout the conceptual design phase and a rapid catch-up effort was not entirely satisfactory. Data ownership (and responsibility) was an issue that never was entirely resolved, and still needs to be if SAP is to be used efficiently.

A final impediment to project progression was the lack of empowerment of some of the business leaders to make decisions on dramatic business procedure changes. Without clear authority to act, some of the leaders were hesitant until late in the project, and many of the procedures that needed to be established came in late.

In the final analysis, upper management commitment, a strong project manager, a motivated staff, and solid methods all contributed to a successful completion within the imposed time-frame.

Managing the Changes

The Human Side of an SAP Implementation

Agreeing to Go Ahead with an SAP Implementation

At the heart of SAP is a presumption that your company will react with vigor (and yes, obedience) to a management dictum that the software be installed and used. However, an SAP implementation will inevitably involve nearly all of your company's staff; thus, the necessity of their 'buying into' the project cannot be overstressed.

This notion of general consensus as a prerequisite for success is not unique to America, but it has been noted by European consultants that implementations over here require more 'buying into' than over there. SAP consultants tend to insist that you need merely to follow the implementation guide, but there is nothing in that guide  that addresses management or staff resistance to the project, nor is there any guidance whatsoever for building consensus and faith in the future system.

It is up to the visionaries to communicate the vision, through meetings, presentations, documents, and seminars. This is true of any major IS undertaking, and doubly true of SAP because of the high level of business involvement. SAP cannot be implemented in a vacuum, behind closed doors. Indeed, SAP tends to kick down doors. And therein lies one of the greater degrees of implementation difficulty.

The Importance of Change Management

Corporations are not democratic institutions. Chief executive officers are not elected by vote of the employees, nor are employees elevated to the ranks of management on merit alone. The dynamics and drama of the staff chart are openly (and in some cases sorely) at the center of any SAP implementation. When business processes are assessed and redrawn, companies find that there are functional rivalries within their organizations and that such rivalries have to be eliminated if the project is to be successful. Such elimination will often include a "redistribution" of employees. It isn't just the desks and filing cabinets that are being rearranged, but the entire scope of the workaday world.

SAP isn't to everyone's taste and not everyone will be pleased to see it coming. Resistance is both normal and predictable, and will be manifested from primarily two sources:

1. the bewildered: those who do not want the company to change from its traditional business process path;

2. the "other" solutionists: those who prefer to acquire and install other software and meld it with beloved legacy systems.

There are three groups of employees most often affected or afflicted:

Middle managers, whose functions are either radically recast or eliminated altogether. Many middle management positions exist to fulfill integration or coordination functions between business groups on a horizontal level. Re-engineered processes and SAP software eliminate much of the need for this.

Because of the reengineering that accompanies an SAP implementation, the system can become a political football, polarizing management into various camps and tribes. To eliminate this factor, project management should double its efforts to communicate with employees during and after the decision-making about processes and roles. Radical changes may not be popular, but they should at least be understood.

Sometimes, middle managers assigned to the reengineering process find that they are obliged to re-order or delete their own positions in the company as part of that process. How could they not resist the project?

IS staff. Traditionally, systems staff have been service-oriented, and it's been a one-way street. Users demand and IS delivers. Whether systems delivery is slow or fast or incomplete or whatever, the systems staff have been viewed as the providers and safekeepers of information flow. There is a negotiation process in which systems people tell users how long it will take to deliver a service (a printout, a screen display, a new system), and usually there is also some give and take as regards the specifications. SAP largely eliminates this negotiation process, and the traditional systems analyst must now more than ever become a business analyst.

Programming and operating system staff will migrate to Basis and ABAP, but only for add-ons and maintenance. The core software of SAP should not be touched, except in the areas referred to as 'user exits'. Never. Fooling with software this integrated will have a boomerang effect. You may think you are tinkering with a stock module only to discover that you have screwed up cash management.

Thus, the importance of internal IS has shifted more than slightly. The information system is now firmly in the hands of those who benefit from it, the business people.

Direct users are a third group that will feel the effects of an SAP implementation because their empowerment (to employ that fat word) is both sudden and irrevocable. It is one thing to enter a sales order to a sales order file. It is another thing to update, with a stroke, the purchasing system, factory scheduling, warehouse inventory, and financial cash flow.

The heightened responsibilities of direct users are in contrast to the lowered (or eliminated) responsibilities of much of middle management. Thus, the change in the company has to be managed, as one class of employee is being buffeted and another elevated.

How to do this is the subject of many other books. Some companies, particularly large ones, attempt to solve the problem by hiring consultants dedicated to change management. These consultants spend a considerable amount of time with 'the bewildereds' and those whose jobs will be changing, smoothing the way for acceptance of new conditions and a new career path.

All the same, eggs are broken en masse to make an SAP omelette, and buzzwords such as *downsizing* or *rightsizing* or *transition smoothing* will be of scant comfort to a number of your employees.

Change management has to be addressed at the onset of any SAP project. Humanity demands it, as should any conscientious management.

ABC of SAP for CEO

Because R/3 can be configured to directly address reengineered business processes, it is often viewed as the perfect partner for a company that is looking to 'streamline', or 're-structure' or 'slim down'. The next word that immediately springs to mind is *downsize*.

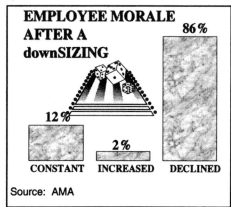

EMPLOYEE MORALE AFTER A downSIZING

86%

12%

2%

CONSTANT   INCREASED   DECLINED

Source: AMA

Please note:

Laying people off is the elimination of jobs with the aim of improving profitability.

Downsizing is the elimination of jobs with the aim of improving profitability.

Rightsizing is the elimination of jobs with the aim of improving profitability.

Call it whatever suits your fancy, but do not think of SAP R/3 as your downsizing partner. By itself, it is only software and will only work according to the way you make it work. And if your down or right sizing project isn't taken as a *result* of clear-headed, strategic business process reengineering and sufficient management action, the exercise will fail, the company will have shed experience and productivity for short-term gain, and the morale of remaining employees will plummet.

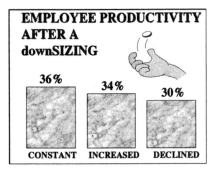

EMPLOYEE PRODUCTIVITY AFTER A downSIZING

36% CONSTANT 34% INCREASED 30% DECLINED

Source: AMA

Having said this, we do understand that a proper implementation of R/3, with a sharp focus on workflow, can result in a serious reduction and/or re-allocation of staff. This is, after all, one of the greatest potential benefits of an SAP R/3 implementation. However, chopped salaries alone do not lead to a fattened bottomed line and implementing SAP with only that thought in mind could lead to heartache at all levels of your company.

Is Evvvrybody Happy? Managing Expectations

There is nothing as bothersome to a manager as employees who assume that things in their department will work, that responsibilities will be clearly laid out, orally and in writing and on wall charts that shunt the sunlight from the windows, and that staff tasks will go box-arrow-box as *planned*. (Our friend and colleague Jim O'Keefe never shuts up about the people from Pompei who surely had plans one night, but that's another story...)   There is nothing more irksome than staff who gabble about 'communication' and 'empowerment'. But

110

listen: carping is a daily constant, for which there is, happily, no remedy. Any manager worth his salt would not want a whole department of Stepford Wives cruising from cubicle to cubicle, mindlessly smiling and mindlessly obeying in carbon copy fashion. So, listen to the complaints, not for their volume, but for their content. Are your people complaining about the working conditions, such as the heating or the lousy coffee. If they are grousing about such items, you aren't in an SAP environment, you are in a company that is going nowhere and you'd best spiffy up your resume and keep one eye on the exit.

If, however, the complaining centers on profitability or, more realistically, *how things might work*, then listen, please, oh please. *How things work* is the key to SAP success. Which is not to say that your staff alone is the key, but, by their chatter, they might be in the mood to make it work.

Clearly, an SAP implementation project is going to leave everyone with expectations of how their business world will look at the end, an open road to glory and profit or a slow trip down slimy stairs to the business cellar.

Upper management assumes that better information will be produced with a faster turnaround. OK, but do they know what information is for and how to use it? If they don't, their expectations may be met by the project, but they won't know it.

Middle management assumes a) it will be downsized (and may be right) and b) intersectional coordination and communication will improve. But how?

Direct Users assume that the new computer system will be a) more complicated, b) faster in terms of response times, c) will eliminate a number of jobs, and d) will be replaced five years hence when either new software or a new CEO comes along.

It is up to you to set the tone. The managing of expectations begins at the outset of the implementation project, while that 'visionary thing' is taking place. You are shooting for the moon, knowing that it is entirely probable you will not get there in the first go. Begin with a simple declaration as to why you are putting in SAP R/3. Make it a mission statement if you are inclined to do such things. But make it clear.

Once the project is launched, communicate your goals far and wide. Establish a project newsletter, hold town meetings (or brown paper bag meetings, or whatever) and articulate your goals to as many employees as possible. You will be putting yourself on the line, but you will have done just as much by launching the project anyway. If you are not able to clearly express the aims of the project, maybe you don't have a clear handle on what they are.

As the project begins in earnest, work with your project manager and your steering committee to see that scope doesn't stretch beyond your goals. If your aims change during the course of an implementation, communicate those changes and make the adjustments without dithering.

Remember that this is an enterprise-wide endeavor and that your staff will be as interested in this implementation as they would be in the implementation of a new pay structure. Consultants will be populating the hallways and workflow charts will be pinned on the walls of conference rooms like LA Dodger pennants. Misapprehensions will naturally abound and will undermine the project if they are not addressed. One worried employee is a case for people skills. A thousand worried employees is a massive loss of production.

As the project roars toward its finish, people will take a long look at what is about to happen and may be taken aback. They will perhaps see fewer of their co-workers in the vicinity and there may still be an excess of those consultants skulking about and looking concerned. You have just entered into the Twilight Zone of change management. SAP R/3 is that eerie Muzak you are hearing in the elevator. Your coffee is a tad more bitter and the receptionist seems to be new and not quite friendly and only marginally attuned to the voice-mail system (are they speaking in East European tongues?). You might tend to come to work fifteen minutes earlier, your tie ten degrees tighter and why doesn't the water fountain work? and you hang around that extra half hour in the evening in case the phone rings for something other than a pizza delivery. Well past sundown, when you leave the building, you will notice a larger number of cigarette butts than usual on the grounds around the exits.

Will it work? Will it work? How will it ever work? (An employee prayer tends to begin with the words "what the hell?"...) To escape that eerie music, those screechy violins, keep your eye on the why of the deal. You, the CEO and you, the CFO. You leaders. You are on the verge of getting what you asked for and your staff needs you to steer a last time through the final shoals. If all you talk about is bottom line, you will find the rocks forthwith. If you have the leadership bones and offer comfort and direction at this point, halleluah. It was your idea. See it through the shoals and onto the shore, with style.

Or bust.

.
.
.
.
.
.
.
.
.
.

The Future of R/3

*How Long Can This Go On? Pushing
the Limits of the System Life Cycle*

How SAP Sends the Hordes into R & D

No software house in history has invested as much in person
years and, by consequence, money, to develop and refine its
product. By the end of 1995, SAP AG was said to have
invested *over seven hundred million dollars* in product
development *since* the first release of R/3 was introduced in
1992. Call it *two hundred and some million a year.* Again,
SAP's figures (which seem to inspire italics) dwarf the
competition. Few software houses have annual revenues of
$200M.

More italics. The newest
release of R/3 is said to have
taken *more than 1000 years of
person effort.* This is what you
call a commitment. What the
world is getting for that
commitment is a continued,
accelerating growth of SAP,
and rapid incorporation of
new ideas into R/3. In 1995, SAP earned 1.8 billion so that

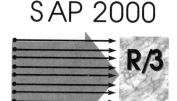

115

would mean $450 million for 1996 R&D if they have stuck to their guns.

With this kind of manpower, SAP has created a niche for itself and is alone. There is no direct competition, no alternative outfit with a complete applications suite that also happens to run in open systems architecture with client/server capacity. In essence, the competition is now of an entirely different nature. Potential clients have to first decide whether or not to run the table with SAP or to consider more traditional options, such as acquisition of multiple other packages and/or another bout of in-house development. SAP quite simply no longer fits on those package selection decision tables in direct comparison to other options.

At the same time, as companies are partnering more and more in the world of systems, SAP finds itself linking elbows with IBM (for the AS/400 platform as well as consulting services), Microsoft (for Windows and the upcoming BackOffice Suite), and one of its own shadow competitors, Oracle (for its data base). There is thus a network around the product bolstering its evolution and its viability.

It is interesting to note that through these fat years, SAP hasn't expanded horizontally, hasn't slipped its tentacles into new and diverse markets. The company's sole activity is the creation and improvement of its software. They have expanded training facilities and course offerings, but have left the majority of consulting business to alliance partners, sometimes for the better and sometimes for the worse. Even the software has remained familiar and uniform. There was talk of an SAP lite, a stripped-down, simpler-to-configure version of the daddy system, but this has not come to fruition, nor is it likely to in the near future.

For the most part, SAP management seems to be focusing more and more on the same points of weakness already noted in this book:

- implementation time and cost

- configuration complexity

- training

For this last point, the effort hasn't yet been entirely a success, but it is clear that the company is addressing its past weaknesses of using a trainers-teach-trainers method. There is such a great demand for experienced implementers and they are nearly all taken up by projects. Very few SAP trainers out there have actual implementation experience. (Ahem, please read the back pages of this book. And excuse the interruption.)

The difficulty remains: anyone with serious SAP experience will be utilized for implementation assistance first, and trainers will, by virtue of supply and demand, remain on a second level.

All the same, this concentration of effort and focus on the single product leads us to believe that the future of SAP is assured until well past the year 2000 and that, for the coming years, the wave of SAP implementations will continue unabated.

What Color is the Smoke?

Watching the movements of SAP (both AG and America) is like Vatican-watching. We often have to read between the lines of the multitude of announcements, ads, and Web page content. Reading tea-leaves is a more exact science and we can't help but shake our collective heads when reading some of the oh-so-certain opinions related in the press.

With so much R&D munchkinpower, SAP tends to announce new wrinkles, new features, and new releases at an alarming and confusing rate. From the fall of 1995 to the spring of 1996, R/3 versions 3.0a, 3.0b, 3.0c, and 3.0d were scattered across the North American SAP fields, all of these representing upgrades from the generally "known" version 2.2. The differences between these versions are important enough to wreak havoc for trainers and implementers if upgrades are not properly monitored and managed. By the time you read this, version 3.1 will have been announced and R/4 itself will be rearing its mysterious head.

Handicapping the features and content of new versions of software is risky. All the same, certain elements that appear to be part and parcel of SAP's future 'look' include:

- internet access (mass proclamations on the Web pages bespeak this);

- the first 'variant' versions of the software (rather than the entire same system at all times);

- continued linking of implementation tools to the IMG;

- object-oriented technology.

On this last point, take a breath. There is supposedly great pressure on SAP to come up with a higher-tech version of this software. The phrase 'cutting edge' is used in the press far too often on this score and since SAP is ultra-sensitive to the press and has felt compelled to answer, there have been ripples and then waves and then currents of ink as regards SAP and its competitors, all having to do with the fact that R/3 is not a fully 'object oriented' piece of work. For those of you who are not up on this facet of computer techno stuff, object orientation allows for a smoother and swifter handling of the system on the part of technicians, or systems folks. What was formerly called 'programming' is heavily affected, as is much of the basic architecture of 'how it works.' This is not an unimportant issue and SAP, with its vast supply of R&D resources, may well be up to the task of converting/upgrading to a fully 'object oriented' state with R/4.

Why? Because of the pressures of techno and biz critics who have columns to write? The need to adhere to up-to-the-minute technology is of huge import when it comes to emerging fields such as the Internet, but is it applicable to established and wider fields such as integrated business applications software? Must an industry leader always employ and integrate 'cutting edge' techniques at the earliest possible moment?

Maybe, just maybe, we are sitting at one of those crossroads left over from the 80's, like the period when TQM and Japanese management techniques were the mantra of the moment.

It might be that the zillions of minutes that SAP can expend on improvements to functions and implementation methods would be far better spent than if they concentrate on answering the academics and the chirps of their (in reality nonexistant) competition.

As Dennis Miller always concludes, I may be wrong and the need to move swiftly to object-oriented technology is a must for SAP and, by extension, its clients. Or object-technology might be the rack-and-pinion steering of its time. Cool, but not the end all be all.

Although there is already talk of R/4, don't expect a major announcement until at least 1998. The shift from R/2 to R/3 is still relatively recent and it is doubtful that SAP, with all of its resources, would be in a position to support three different versions of its integrated software suite. Instead, we can look forward to new releases of R/3 at a fairly steady pace.

The Same Music with New Instruments

There have been continuous rumblings for some time about SAP's having targeted the mid-range market and one obvious sector is the aging distributed networks 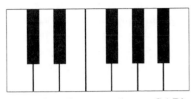 of minicomputers. This huge market has not been SAP's playing field in North America. Roughly 70% of the companies using SAP in the U.S. are of the Fortune 500 set and the perception is that SAP is a big boy's toy. It is a perception that SAP has aggressively tried to counter, not because of marketing desires, but because it is not so. Remember the figures we gave you earlier? As of Sapphire '95, R/3 had been sold into 1105 large companies (revenues over $1B), 771 medium-sized companies ($250M to $1B), and 1337 small companies ($5M to $250M).

All the same, SAP announced new platforms in 1996, the most tantalizing of which is the AS/400.

There are a number of major considerations if SAP is to succeed in this market, among them:

- Support

  With its strategy of remaining a software factory and leaving implementation and training to alliance partners, how much support will SAP be able to provide to potentially thousands of new (smaller) clients?

- Support (again)

  With so many huge and important existing clients, won't SAP be geared toward their functions and profiles rather than to the smaller clients?

- Pricing

    How will SAP be situated vis-à-vis the competition?

- Consulting

    How will smaller companies afford the high ratio of consulting costs to software costs? And, with an already absorbed consulting base, where do these companies turn?

- Implementation

    Smaller companies will have a harder time allocating staff to an SAP project on a full-time basis.

One single answer to each of these concerns has been provided through a series of SAP announcements and clarifications: the intent to provide pre-configured systems or, at worst, a package with 100 or so basic business processes to choose from. Older systems people (anyone over forty, at least) will remember the buzz word of the early 1980's in just this regard: turnkey systems. Just start 'er up, sonny, and keep an eye on the speedometer.

All the same, if SAP can provide viable answers to the above questions, the mid-range world will never be the same.

......

Last Minute Notes

A Rapid Once-over of Related Subjects
That Barely Fit in an Apprentice Guide

EIS - Executive Information System

SAP now offers tools for the development of a separate data base dedicated to a "top of the pyramid" reporting facility for high level managers. The advantage of having an EIS is the speed and ease of use, but only if the data base has been properly set up to begin with.

The basic features of an EIS are:

- multi-dimensional attributes, such as customer, products regions, and departments;

- a hierarchy to many of the attributes and drill-down reporting (or we could just say multi-level reporting) within the hierarchy;

- reports are displayed in a variety of formats, such as spreadsheets, charts, and graphs.

Implementation of an EIS will require a database administrator and perhaps an analyst or two. Completion (or the promise of) such a subproject can do wonders towards gaining over-all project support from high level managers.

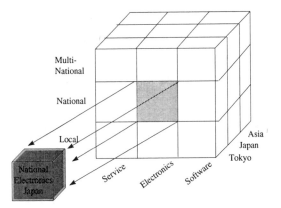

EDI - Electronic Data Interchange

Legend has it that when Dr. Naismith invented basketball, the game was played for some months or years with a peach basket that still had its bottom. Each time a basket was scored, someone had to climb up a ladder and remove the ball.

The rise of electronic data interchange (thanks to the development of international data standards) is comparable to the removal of that peach basket bottom. Should have been done years ago, but here we are at last.

With EDI, SAP users can exchange data with partners, clients, suppliers, whoever has a system with data that can be used by SAP. The EDI interface can trigger functions within SAP applications for instant processing or hold incoming data for manual processing that requires human intervention.

A system that involves massive data entry can be radically streamlined with an intensive EDI effort. Data sharing and communications should be a central factor in the re-engineering process, since the benefits are so obvious and so immediate.

ABAP/4 Development Workbench

The workbench is a set of related development tools for the development of new applications or the enhancement of existing SAP applications. This workbench includes:

- Editor

- Screen and Menu Painters

- Interactive Debugger

- Computer-aided test tools

- Development tools using dynpro technology

- ABAP/4 Dictionary

- Enterprise data model

This is only a partial list. Suffice to say, development of add-on applications can be done by a developer without detailed background concerning the hardware or data base. The tools cover the entirety of the gamut of software development, from conception to development to testing and installation.

Note: Dynpro is an SAP term for "dynamic program", which includes, in one go, screen setup, the processing of fields, and field testing procedures. Unless you are on the IS side of the river, forget you just read this.

Riding into the Sunrise

So? Any Questions?

Writing about SAP is a hazardous activity. Each day, there are new announcements on the Internet, (HTTP://www.sap.com) more elements to cover, more ambitions being expressed, and the debates rage in the business press and in conference rooms around the world: is R/3 a dream or a nightmare? Can it be implemented without hocking the company cars? Will it work on the AS/400 or not? Is the Aris Toolset worth using or merely a pricey toy? How many consultants do we need and where will we find them? What does Object Link Embedding mean to our bottom line?

Obviously, only some of the answers are to be found in this book. Answers to the million other questions will have to be found both at SAP itself, with consultants, and within your own enterprise. The SAP river flows fast **and** deep, so be sure to keep asking questions even when you think you have all the answers.

While riding the SAP river, you may need an oar or two. We don't have all the answers ourselves, and it is our job to find them however we can. In that light, feel free to grab an oar and check us out at www.tcall.com

TERMS AND ACRONYMS

ABAP	Advanced Business Application Programming Language
AM	Fixed Assets Management application in SAP
ASAP	No, we say *an* SAP
Business Process	a group or series of activities by which inputs are turned to outputs that benefit the customer
C/S	Client/server
CO	Controlling application in SAP R/3
Configure	to configure SAP is to set the options in the tables for your company.
Customize	making changes to the system that will fit your process designs
FI	Financial application in SAP R/3
Gap analysis	the analysis of what you want to do that you think won't be provided by SAP
GUI	Graphical User Interface
HR	Human Resources application in SAP R/3
ICOE	Industry Centers of Expertise
Interfaces	Program-driven connections between disparate data bases
IS	Information systems
IS	Industry Solutions application in SAP
IT	Information technology
Middleware (Basis)	The / between client and server, as in Client/Server
MM	Materials management application in R/3
OC	Office & Communications application in SAP R/3
OR	Organization & Reengineering Partner OR Partner
PM	Production Maintenance application in SAP R/3
Portability	the capacity of software to be run on various operating systems
PP	Production Planning application in SAP R/3
PS	Project System application in SAP R/3
PTA	Parent Teachers Association
QA	Quality Assurance in SAP R/3
QM	Quality Management application in SAP R/3
RMD	the author's initials
SAP	Ess Ay Pee
SD	Sales and distribution application in SAP R/3
Software suite	multiple software applications derived from common design

About **The Consulting Alliance:**

The Consulting Alliance is a single-source firm offering total services to companies seeking to implement and use SAP products. Its consulting group is known as **THE OR PARTNER GROUP,** which means "Organization and Reengineering Partner". Our consultant profile is an average age of 35, with 4 ½ years of SAP experience preceded by eleven years of industry experience. We offer total solution consulting, from strategic services to implementation consulting and end user training.

We follow SAP's guidelines for implementation according to a project approach that has been approved by SAP.

We are outcome-oriented and underscore the **transfer of SAP knowledge** from our staff to client staff during implementation project and through **THE DOLPHIN GROUP** educational services.

We believe that SAP education is the essential missing link to successful R/3 implementations and that a transfer of SAP knowledge from ourselves to our clients is the most useful service we can provide. By complementing SAP applications courses, we strive for client self-sufficiency and, ultimately, client independence. THE DOLPHIN GROUP, with facilities in Wilmington, DE and the Bahamas, offers seminars and training at all levels: executive-level, project managers, coordinators, and direct users. Our instructors are consultants who have distinguished themselves in the field and all have legitimate SAP implementation experience and background.

- In the Path of the *Whirlwind*™: An Executive Course in SAP R/3.

- Capturing the *Whirlwind*™: Your Field Guide for a Successful SAP R/3 Implementation.

- Acquisition Decision and Support Program.

- Dolphin Bootcamp 101: 10 days of hands-on training from FI-CO to SD-MM and an integration test during which students build and test a functioning model company in R/3.

- Dolphin Bootcamp 201: a configuration and integration workshop; 10 days of learning by doing: students learn to configure an R/3 system (FI, CO, SD, MM, PP, and HR) by building a functional model based upon a case study.

The Consulting Alliance is pleased to announce the upcoming publication of

Capturing the *Whirlwind*, Your Field Guide to a Successful R/3 Implementation

This book will be invaluable to project managers, module leaders, super users, and anyone actively associated with an SAP R/3 implementation. It is intended to complement our previous book, In the Path of the *Whirlwind*, An Apprentice Guide to the World of SAP. Some of the chapters:

- The Best Use of Scouts and Mercenaries, Getting the Most Out of Your Consultants
- Distinguishing North from South, The Pitfalls of the Gap Analysis, AS IS, and Other Consulting Phases
- Of Saints and Savages, The (In)human side of an Implementation
- Bird Calls and Animal Wails, How to Identify Resistance and Make It Your Ally
- Only You Can Prevent Forest Fires, How Scope Ignites During SAP Implementations

The book will be available in early December of 1996, but can be ordered now through The Consulting Alliance. To order:

In the Path of the *Whirlwind*, An Apprentice Guide to the World of SAP

Capturing the *Whirlwind*, Your Field Guide to a Successful SAP R/3 Implementation (due December 1996)

QUANTITY ORDERS - ANY TITLE				BOTH TITLES			
1-10	$22.95	50-99	$19.95	1-10	$39.95	50-99	$35.95
11-50	$20.95	100+	$18.95	11-50	$36.95	100+	$34.95
plus shipping costs				We accept VISA and Mastercard			

Contact us at:

The CONSULTING ALLIANCE, L.L.C.
101 South Main Avenue, 6th Fl
Sioux Falls, SD, USA 57104-6423

Phone (605) 339-3074 or (888) 466-8244
Internet: www.tcall.com